THE HAMMARSKJOLD FORUMS

The First in a Series of Case Studies on the Role
of Law in the Settlement of International Disputes

THE ISSUES IN THE BERLIN-GERMAN CRISIS

Robert R. Bowie
James Bryant Conant
Eli Whitney Debevoise

John J. McCloy
George B. Munroe
Frederick A. O. Schwarz

1962

The Background Papers and Proceedings of the
First Hammarskjöld Forum Organized by
THE ASSOCIATION OF THE BAR OF THE
CITY OF NEW YORK
Lyman M. Tondel, Jr., Editor

Published by
OCEANA PUBLICATIONS, INC.
DOBBS FERRY, NEW YORK
1963

Library of Congress Catalog Card Number: 63-14451

Printed in the United States of America

THE ASSOCIATION OF THE BAR OF THE CITY OF NEW YORK

Orison S. Marden, President   1960-1962
Herbert Brownell, President   1962-

COMMITTEE
on
THE LAWYER'S ROLE IN THE SEARCH FOR PEACE

Lyman M. Tondel, Jr., Chairman

The Honorable Dudley B. Bonsal   Carlyle E. Maw
George W. Haight   Robert M. Pennoyer

Frederick A. O. Schwarz

THE STAFF

Crawford Shaw, Fellow of the Association, 1961-1962
Edward R. Bendet, Fellow of the Association, 1962-1963
Arthur A. Charpentier, Librarian of the Association
Joseph L. Andrews, Reference Librarian
Anthony P. Grech, Assistant Reference Librarian

NOTES

It is obviously impossible to keep material of the sort contained in these volumes current. Those who use them for educational purposes should themselves bring the material up to date. The work involved in so doing can only make the material more meaningful to themselves and to those who learn from them.

The Working Paper that appears in this Volume was distributed in connection with the first Hammarskjöld Forum.

ACKNOWLEDGEMENT

In addition to inspiring this series of Forums, James N. Rosenberg of the New York Bar made a substantial financial contribution which enabled the Association to embark on the project. A grant was made by The Ford Foundation early in 1963 to enable the series to continue and a portion of the earlier cost had been met by a grant from the Ottinger Foundation, Inc.

TABLE OF CONTENTS

Preface

In 1960-61 The Association of the Bar of the City of New York was forcefully reminded by two of its senior members, James N. Rosenberg and Grenville Clark, that it should be devoting more of its resources and attention to the cause of world peace through law. It was not that it had by any means defaulted in this field of law, but rather that none of its existing committees or activities was intended to concentrate on the primary challenge to lawyers in our day — namely, the role of law in the settlement of international disputes.

After exploring numerous possibilities it was concluded to conduct, as forums, a series of case studies. It was deliberately decided to consider disputes of the first magnitude, involving political, military, economic and social, as well as legal, problems. It was understood that existing law might be found to play a minor role in these controversies. Yet it was felt that the role of law, whatever it might be, should be more fully appreciated because if there is to be meaningful progress towards international disarmament and the elimination of war as a means of settling international disputes, then means of settlement alternate to war — means under law — must be developed.

It was recognized that under the spur of ever more devastating weapons, there have been in the last 70 years a series of significant steps in the development of peaceful means for settling international controversies — including the Hague Conventions; the League of Nations and the Permanent Court of International Justice; the United Nations and the International Court of Justice; the Organization of American States; and the Court of Justice of the European Economic Community. These steps have not, however, prevented war. In this sense they have all failed.

Yet, in a larger sense, these efforts may not have failed. World law may be impractical, or impossible of achievement at this stage of human history, but these steps and others may have marked the way towards some of the elements of a world at peace under law. They certainly have reflected, and helped induce, a far more extensive consideration of the problems of peacefully settling international disputes than ever before. And they have had results that should be more generally known. For example, in only one adversary case decided by the Permanent Court of International Justice or the International Court of Justice has the losing nation failed to abide by the Court's decision; and all of the rulings of the Court of Justice of the European Economic Community, many of which have involved economic matters of major concern to the disputants, have been carried out. The United Nations has prevented wars. There has, through all this, been a sort of common law development of the means of peaceful settlement of international disputes even though wars and rumors of war still fill the air.

Accordingly it was concluded that it might be useful, and should surely be educational, for there to be a series of case studies in the role of law in settling international disputes, and three forums were held in 1962 at the House of the Association in New York City. A fourth is in the planning stage as this is written. The first considered the Berlin-German crisis; the second, the United Nations action in the Congo; and the third, the Cuban crisis of October, 1962. The first three volumes of this series are on these three subjects. Each volume contains (1) an outstanding Working Paper, prepared by a prominent legal scholar in the field, which summarizes, but with appropriate detail, the legal and factual background of the dispute; (2) a condensation of the discussion at the Forum by the author of the Working Paper and commentators who included leading participants in the affairs discussed; and (3) an extensive bibliography prepared by the Research Staff of the Association's Library. Due to the unique access of the Association to the United Nations, to national leaders, and to prominent legal scholars, the participants have been notable.

As previously indicated, it was recognized in planning this series that such major disputes as those in Berlin, the Congo and Cuba could not, in practice, be solved exclusively under existing legal methods and that, in any event, rights and duties under law comprised only part of the problem in each case. Yet it clearly appeared at the Forums that the nations involved did have legal rights and duties; that even the Soviet Union seeks to justify, and with great particularity, its actions in the name of law and, for all we know, may even have rejected some courses of action for which even their apologists could not rationalize any legal justification; that rules, or at least patterns, of conduct by nations, by groups of nations, and by the United Nations, are being constantly developed, as in the Congo and in the Inter-American system; and that the experience being acquired in peacefully trying to solve these disputes must be understood if progress is to be made.

If, as we must hope, fear of nuclear devastation is to drive the nations into finding means of peacefully solving controversies with each other, the search for such means can only be hastened by greater understanding of what actions, ambitions, needs or ideologies lead to critical disputes; of what procedures and devices have helped solve such disputes, and what have not; of what new law is evolving in connection with efforts to solve such disputes; of the extent to which rulers have had regard for at least the pretext of legality; and of what sanctions and obligations have restrained them the most.

As the original planning of this series neared completion, Dag Hammarskjöld, an honorary member of the Association, was tragically killed in the course of a mission of peace. As a memorial to him the series was entitled "The Hammarskjöld Forums." Adlai E. Stevenson, United States Permanent Representative to the United Nations, and his Deputy, Francis T. P. Plimpton, inaugurated the Forums at the first meeting which was devoted to a consideration of the Berlin-German crisis. Remarks made by them on that occasion are included in Volume I.

Before the second Forum, on April 30, 1962, on The Legal Aspects of the United Nations Action in the Congo, His Excellency U Thant, Acting Secretary-General of the United Nations, dedicated to Dag Hammarskjöld's memory The Hammarskjöld Room in the House of The Association of the Bar of the City of New York. His dedication is included in Volume II.

In publishing these volumes it is hoped by the Association that each will provide some of those who conduct public discussions, as well as some students and teachers, with background information on a specific controversy; that each will alert the reader to the existing and developing law involved in the particular controversy; and that all who read may thereby become more aware that only by the substitution of the rule of law may war be eliminated as the ultimate means of settling international disputes.

Lyman M. Tondel, Jr.

Inauguration of the Hammarskjold Forums

Remarks
of
The Honorable Adlai E. Stevenson

To inaugurate the Hammarskjöld Forum is an honor which I assume with great pleasure. He was one of those men — and it has been my good fortune to know him from the time he arrived here, and even to be present at his funeral in Uppsala— who tried to fill in the gap between the past and the present. During his tenure of office, Mr. Hammarskjöld displayed a great vision — based on a conviction of purpose tempered by keen appreciation of practical reality — of peaceful change in this turbulent world. The legal framework within which he sought to express his conviction was, of course, the Charter of the United Nations. In the introduction to his last Annual Report on the work of the United Nations, the late Secretary-General and posthumous Nobel Peace Prize Laureate has provided us with a penetrating analysis of his views of the role of the Organization. I would commend it to all of you.

Mr. Hammarskjöld stressed that the paramount and ultimate aim of the United Nations has been and remains "to save succeeding generations from the scourge of war." He spoke of what he called the three principles found in the Charter as a means to that end: equal political rights, equal economic opportunities, and the rule of law.

The Secretary-General also pointed out that the Charter drew a further logical conclusion from the ultimate aims of the Organization as well as from these three principles: it outlawed the use of force, "save in the common interest." It may be readily agreed that the question under what circumstances the Charter permits the use of armed force is one to which the answer, even today, can only be rudimentary, at best. The Charter permits the use of force in certain circumstances pursuant to a decision by the Security

Council. It also recognizes the exercise of the inherent right of individual or collective self-defense if an armed attack occurs against a member of the United Nations, at least until the Security Council has taken measures necessary to maintain international peace and security.

Sixteen years have not been sufficient to allow the Organization to chart definitively the criteria under which, pursuant to the Charter, the use of force is permissible. It is questionable whether it will ever be possible definitively to chart such criteria. Nevertheless, it is entirely clear that, if this Organization is to be a dynamic instrument of Governments, through which they can work together for the promotion of the purposes and principles of the Charter, the use of force can be no longer a recognized means of achieving national ends. Such a use of force would be contrary to the principles of the Organization and would not be "in the common interest." The Organization itself may authorize the use of force to maintain or restore international peace and security, but not for lesser causes.

The world is witness today to an explosive rise in expectations; political, economic, social and educational. These expectations continually give rise to demands. How often they strain the resources upon which the demands are made, we well know. To satisfy these expectations requires patient, and, above all, peaceful adjustments. The United Nations has been designed to make such adjustments possible. What it requires is a recognition by the members that the use of armed force for national ends — or even for some international ends — no matter for what illusory short term gain, is really no gain at all in the end, for it is destructive of the very principles of the Charter which provide for equality and justice to all Members in a changing world. It is as destructive of the life of the Charter as it is of the life of man.

The Charter provides the most extensive machinery ever contrived for the peaceful settlement of disputes and for the adjustment of differences among states. The members of the United Nations are bound to avail themselves of this machinery, and not to resort to their own measures when this machinery does not provide a quick, or a desired result. In view of the alternatives that exist, with the ever-growing potential of modern arms, I submit that it is today imperative to rely, at every turn, on the principles of the Charter, and to use to the full the machinery and processes of the United Nations for effecting peaceful change. The use of that machinery must be imaginative and persevering. It may not produce immediate results. But if it results in an expanding role for law in the settlement of disputes, then reliance on the Charter will have given much to us all.

If these forums should result in expanding understanding of this machinery and of the law, then they also will have given much to us all.

Extract from Remarks

of

The Honorable

Francis T. P. Plimpton

I am just going to add a footnote, and the footnote is about Hammarskjöld.

One can just see that imperturbable figure with those icy blue eyes, smoking a long thin cigar, sitting and listening to this sort of a forum, and one can sense the quiet appreciation of that dedicated international civil servant of what this Association is doing, because if there ever has been in this world an embodiment of the principles and the practice of international law and international order, it was Hammarskjöld.

This forum would have delighted him, and I am sure that in some place, I know not where, he is smiling his imperturbable smile at us now and wishing that the dedication to international law that is being evidenced in this building this evening would spread six and a half blocks over into the East River structure where it is so sorely needed.

Forum Program

and

Identification of Participants

The Issues in the Berlin-German Crisis

JANUARY 29, 1962

INTRODUCTION
ORISON S. MARDEN, ESQ.
President of The Association of the Bar of the City of New York

INAUGURATION OF THE HAMMARSKJÖLD FORUMS
H. E. MR. ADLAI E. STEVENSON
United States Permanent Representative to the United Nations
H. E. MR. FRANCIS T. P. PLIMPTON
United States Deputy Permanent Representative to the United Nations

THE POLITICAL AND LEGAL BACKGROUND OF THE BERLIN-GERMAN CRISIS
PROFESSOR ROBERT R. BOWIE
Director of the Center for International Affairs, Harvard University, and General Counsel to the United States High Commissioner for Germany, 1950-1951

THE LEGAL ASPECTS OF THE BERLIN-GERMAN CRISIS
ELI WHITNEY DEBEVOISE, ESQ.
General Counsel to the United States High Commissioner for Germany, 1951-1953, and Acting Deputy United States High Commissioner for Germany, 1952-1953
GEORGE B. MUNROE, ESQ.
Office of General Counsel, United States High Commission, 1951-1953; Justice, United States Court of Restitution Appeals of the Allied High Commission for Germany, 1953-1954

COMMENTS

DR. JAMES B. CONANT
United States High Commissioner for Germany, 1953-1954 and United States Ambassador to the Federal Republic of Germany, 1955-1957
JOHN J. McCLOY, ESQ.
Assistant Secretary of War, 1941-1945; United States Military Governor and United States High Commissioner for Germany, 1949-1952; until recently Advisor to the President on Disarmament.
FREDERICK A. O. SCHWARZ, ESQ.
General Counsel to the United States High Commissioner for Germany, 1953-1954.

GENERAL DISCUSSION FROM THE FLOOR

CONCLUSION

LYMAN M. TONDEL, JR., ESQ.
Chairman, Committee on the Lawyer's Role in the Search for Peace

Working Paper: The Legal Background of the Berlin-German Crisis.*

I. Origin and Development of Western Legal Rights in Berlin

The right of the United States, the United Kingdom, and France, as of the U.S.S.R., to occupy and control any part of Germany, including Berlin, derives from the total defeat of the German armed forces, the unconditional surrender of Germany, and the assumption by the four powers jointly of supreme authority in respect of Germany on June 5, 1945.[1]** After those events Germany had to comply with any requirements which the four powers which had jointly assumed supreme authority might impose upon it. Between themselves the four powers had made arrangements respecting the joint occupation and control of conquered Germany. June 5, 1945 was the day upon which binding agreements embodying these arrangements might enter into operation.

A. *Allied Planning for Quadripartite Occupation and Control*

Allied intentions for defeated Germany appear to have been governed by the decision first made early in the war that German surrender would have to be unconditional.[2] Although the country was not to be annexed, the Nazi régime was to be destroyed; hence the task of governing Germany during the occupation period would devolve entirely upon the victorious allies. Berlin then, transportation and communications center of Germany and repository of the records and files of what had been a highly centralized Nazi administration, was the logical seat for the joint Allied authority which was to govern Germany.[3] Special arrangements for the joint occupation and administration of Greater Berlin, an area of occupation separate from the zonal divisions of Germany as a whole, appear in

*This paper was prepared by Miss Doris Carroll, Research Assistant at the Harvard Law School, under the direction of Professor Robert R. Bowie.

**All footnotes are on pages 65-80.

the first of the agreements between the Western powers and the Soviet Union respecting the occupation and administration of conquered Germany prepared by the European Advisory Commission.[4] The September 12, 1944 Protocol on Zones of Occupation in Germany and Administration of Greater Berlin[5] provided that, for the purposes of occupation, Germany would be divided into three zones, one to be allotted to each power, "and a special Berlin area, which will be under joint occupation by the three Powers."[6] Paragraph 5 of the Protocol reads:

> An Inter-Allied Governing Authority (Komendatura) consisting of three Commandants, appointed by their respective Commanders-in-Chief, will be established to direct jointly the administration of the "Greater Berlin" Area.

The second major accord between the powers on postwar arrangements for defeated Germany was the November 14, 1944 Agreement on Control Machinery in Germany.[7] Supreme authority in Germany was to be exercised, on instructions from their respective governments, by the American, British, and Soviet commanders-in-chief, each in his own zone of occupation, and also jointly in matters affecting Germany as a whole.[8] The three commanders-in-chief, acting together as a body, would constitute the Control Council, whose decisions were to be unanimous.[9] The Control Council had among its functions to ensure appropriate uniformity of action by the commanders-in-chief in their respective zones of occupation, to initiate plans and reach agreed decisions on the chief questions affecting Germany as a whole, to control the German central administration when one was established, and to direct the administration of Greater Berlin through appropriate organs.[10] Provisions for the administration of Berlin are contained in Article 7, paragraphs (a) and (b), of the Agreement: an Inter-Allied Governing Authority (in Russian, *Komendatura*) consisting of three commandants, one from each power, was to be established to direct jointly the administration of the Greater Berlin area, the *Komendatura* to be assisted by a technical staff which was to supervise and control the activities of the local organs of Greater Berlin responsible for its municipal services.

The Agreement on Control Machinery in Germany, unlike the

2

Protocol on Zones of Occupation and Administration of Berlin, contains a provision with respect to its duration:

> The Allied organs for the control and administration of Germany outlined above will operate during the initial period of the occupation of Germany immediately following surrender, that is, the period when Germany is carrying out the basic requirements of unconditional surrender.[11]

Article 11 of that Agreement recites that "the question of the Allied organs required for carrying out the functions of control and administration in Germany in a later period" was to be the subject of a separate agreement between the Allied powers.

At Yalta in February, 1945, the Heads of Government of the United States, the United Kingdom, and the U.S.S.R. issued a communiqué stating that the three had agreed upon a plan for coordinated administration and control of Germany "through a central Control Commission consisting of the Supreme Commanders of the Three Powers with headquarters in Berlin."[12] The specific provisions of the European Advisory Commission agreements were not made publicly known, however, until June 5, 1945, when statements of them were issued simultaneously with the Declaration Regarding the Defeat of Germany and the Assumption of Supreme Authority by the Allied Powers.[13]

No express provisions concerning access to the joint occupation area of Berlin through the eastern zone of Germany to be occupied by Soviet forces appear in any of the formal war-time agreements concluded between the United States, the United Kingdom, and the Soviet Union. On the occasion of the 1948 blockade of Berlin the Western powers were to state that: "These agreements implied the right of free access to Berlin."[14] The first specific expression of an understanding that American and British occupying troops were to be able to move freely to and from their respective occupation zones to Berlin appears in the correspondence between President Truman, Prime Minister Churchill, and Premier Stalin on June 14-18, 1945 concerning redistribution of troops to their respective zones of occupation and concurrent movement of Western occupying forces into Berlin. The areas occupied by the Allied armies at the cessation of hostilities in May, 1945, did not correspond to the

3

zones of occupation laid down in the agreements adopted by the European Advisory Commission; while the Soviet army was in sole and complete occupation of Berlin, the British and American forces had penetrated far into the area which was to constitute the Soviet zone of occupation.[15] When on June 5, 1945 representatives of the supreme commands of the United States, the United Kingdom, France, and the U.S.S.R. met in Berlin to sign and issue the instruments on initial occupation and control of Germany, Marshal Zhukov maintained that Allied troops should be redistributed into their prescribed occupation zones before Western forces could enter Berlin for joint occupation and organization of the Allied control machinery for Germany. The four commanders-in-chief agreed to refer the question to their respective governments for decision.[16] In consequence, President Truman on June 14, 1945 sent a message to Premier Stalin in which he proposed, should Stalin agree, to order the withdrawal of American troops to their zone of occupation beginning on June 21, 1945:

> in accordance with arrangements between the respective commanders, including in these arrangements simultaneous movement of the national garrisons into Greater Berlin and provision of free access by air, road, and rail from Frankfurt and Bremen to Berlin for U.S. forces.[17]

Prime Minister Churchill sent a similar message to Stalin on June 15, 1945.[18] Stalin replied to Truman on June 16, 1945, and in much the same terms to Churchill on June 17, 1945, with a request only that the date of troop redeployment be postponed to July 1, 1945. Stalin's message concluded: "On our part all necessary measures will be taken in Germany . . . in accordance with the above-stated plan."[19] On June 29, 1945, General Clay and General Weeks, representing respectively the American and British military commanders, met with Marshal Zhukov in Berlin to make arrangements for the taking over of Berlin and the withdrawal of Allied forces to their allotted occupation zones. General Clay so recounts some of that day's discussion:

> We had explained our intent to move into Berlin utilizing three rail lines and two highways and such air space as we needed. Zhukov would not recognize that these routes were essential and point-

4

ed out that the demobilization of Soviet forces was taxing existing facilities. I countered that we were not demanding exclusive use of these routes but merely access over them without restrictions other than the normal traffic control and regulations which the Soviet administration would establish for its own use. General Weeks supported my contention strongly. . . . We did not wish to accept specific routes which might be interpreted as a denial of our right of access over all routes but there was merit to the Soviet contention that existing routes were needed for demobilization purposes. . . . Therefore Weeks and I accepted as a temporary arrangement the allocation of a main highway and rail line and two air corridors, reserving the right to reopen the question in the Allied Control Council. . . . While no record was kept at this meeting, I dictated my notes that evening and they include the following:

It was agreed that all traffic — air, road and rail, . . . would be free from border search or control by customs or military authorities.[20]

The withdrawal of American and British forces from parts of Mecklenburg, Saxony, Thuringia, and Anhalt in the Soviet zone began on July 1, 1945 concurrently with the start of Western garrisons for entry into Berlin, as the Heads of Government had agreed and the military generals had arranged.

A second meeting between General Clay, General Weeks, and Marshal Zhukov took place in Berlin on July 7, 1945, at which questions pertinent to Berlin were decided. The Berlin *Komendatura* was established, its resolutions on "questions of principle and problems common to all zones [*sic*]" to require the unanimous approval of all four sector commandments.[21] It was agreed that transportation and movement within Berlin were to be unrestricted between the sectors.[22] Problems about the provision of food and fuel for the city were also resolved. Zhukov insisted that coal for Berlin be made available from the Ruhr, and that the Western powers supply food sufficient to support the civilian population of the western sectors of the city. The traditional food sources for Berlin had been the surrounding country and agricultural provinces in the Soviet zone, but General Clay agreed to accept responsibility for bringing in food for the inhabitants of the American

5

sector, subject to the establishment of a common ration in all sectors of Berlin. General Weeks was to obtain his government's agreement that the United Kingdom would ensure provision of food for the British sector, and from the British zone a fair proportion of the coal necessary to supply Berlin.[23] The West has in fact ensured supply of food and fuel to the civilian population of the Western sectors of Berlin since July 15, 1945.[24]

On July 11, 1945, the Berlin *Komendatura* held its first meeting. A city administration under a Soviet-appointed executive Magistrat had already been established for all of Berlin during the initial period of exclusive Russian occupation, and was in operation. The first order of the Allied *Komendatura* was to continue in force all existing regulations and ordinances which had been issued by the Soviet Military Administration and by the Magistrat during the time of sole Soviet occupation.[25]

The Heads of Government of the United States, the United Kingdom, and the U.S.S.R. met in conference at Potsdam, near Berlin, from July 17 until August 2, 1945, *inter alia* to formulate a coordinated Allied policy toward defeated Germany during the period of Allied control. A Council of Foreign Ministers was established, one of the functions of which was "the preparation of a peace settlement for Germany to be accepted by the Government of Germany when a government adequate for the purpose is established."[26] Political and economic principles to govern the treatment of Germany in the initial control period were agreed upon. Politically, militarism and Nazism were to be eliminated, and the administration in Germany was to be directed toward structural decentralization and the development of local responsibility. "For the time being" no central German government was to be formed, but inasmuch as Germany was to be treated as a single economic unit, certain German administrative departments were to be established, "particularly in the fields of finance, transport, communications, foreign trade and industry," to act under the direction of the Control Council.[27] Economically, Germany's war potential was to be eliminated, as was its "present excessive concentration of economic power" exemplified by cartels and other monopolistic arrangements. But during the period of occupation Germany was to be treated as a single economic unit, and to this end common policies were to be established concerning, *inter alia*, mining and industrial production and its allocation; import and export programs for Germany as a whole; currency and banking; reparation and removal of industrial war potential; and transportation and communications.[28] Part III of the Potsdam Protocol is specifically concerned with reparations from Germany, but provisions with respect to reparations appear as well in the Economic Principles section of the Protocol.

On August 30, 1945, the commanders-in-chief of the armed forces in Germany of the United States, the United Kingdom, the U.S.S.R., and France, acting jointly as members of the Control Council, issued Proclamation No. 1 announcing that the Control Council had been established in virtue of the supreme authority and powers assumed by the four governments in their Declaration of June 5, 1945, and that supreme authority in matters affecting Germany as a whole had been conferred upon the Control Council.[29]

B. *The Breakdown of Quadripartite Control*

The general arrangements for access to Berlin for Western occupying forces by road, rail, and air made between Marshal Zhukov and Generals Clay and Weeks on June 29, 1945 were further defined in succeeding months through actions of the Allied control machinery in Germany. It was agreed that Western military personnel and military freight might use the Helmstedt-Berlin railroad track through the Soviet zone, and the Marienborn-Berlin *Autobahn* route.[30] The number of air corridors to Berlin to be available for use by the Western powers was increased to three in November, 1945. "Flight over these routes will be conducted without previous notice being given, by aircraft of the nations governing Germany."[31] Barge traffic into Berlin was the subject of separate agreements between the British and Soviet zones.[32] Until March 30, 1948 authorized military passenger and freight traffic moved over these routes to and from Berlin without other restriction than compliance with established and reasonable traffic and safety regulations.[33]

7

As the original purpose of the zones was to mark off the areas of occupation of the four occupying powers, zonal frontiers were not initially intended or used to restrict movement of Germans within Germany.[34] In the first months of the occupation, transport routes and facilities were, necessarily, used by and for the occupying forces. The German railroad system, Berlin its center, had come out of the war in a remarkably sound state, but extensive dismantling of track and installations and the taking of rolling stock for reparations were immediately instituted in the Soviet zone. What facilities remained were preempted in large measure for the transport of reparations to Russia. With economic revival in the Soviet zone, transport came increasingly to be dedicated to commercial interzonal trade.[35] By 1948 commercial passenger and freight traffic was moving freely between Berlin and the Western zones over all highway and rail routes, and from the British zone by inland waterway as well.[36] The three air corridors to Berlin were being used by civil airlines of the Allied powers for commercial flights, as well as by Western military aircraft. On March 6, 1946, the United States member of the Coordinating Committee of the Allied control authority had submitted a memorandum discussing the need for additional air corridors for commercial aviation, as the three established corridors were deemed insufficient for safe, economical operation of aircraft over Germany. The problem was referred to the Air Directorate, where on April 30, 1946 the Soviet delegate would not agree to the extension of existing air corridors because:

> The Soviet Delegation thinks that the existing system of air routes through the Soviet Zone of Occupation in Germany is fully sufficient, not only to meet the requirements of the Allied Troops in the Sector of Greater Berlin, but also to carry out successfully all the Allied transportation needs for commercial cargoes regardless of their volume.[37]

In the broader area of economic reconstruction, however, quadripartite administration of Germany as a whole began early to falter. No progress was ever to be made by the Control Council in establishing plans for the pooling of the industrial resources of the several zones or for common export and import programs.[38] In the absence of economic unity for Germany as a whole, the United States in 1946 proposed to bring about the economic fusion of the American zone with any other zone or zones.[39] Its offer was accepted by the United Kingdom, and the two zones treated thereafter as a single area for all economic purposes.[40] By 1947 the West had been charging for some time that the Soviet Union was obstructing economic unity in Germany and was taking illegal and excessive reparations.[41] In its turn, the U.S.S.R. blamed German economic disunity on Western intransigence and encouragement of separatist movements, and accused the Western powers of failing to deliver the Soviet Union's share of reparations from their zones.[42] At the fifth session of the Council of Foreign Ministers in November and December, 1947, the Soviet Union pressed for the immediate establishment of a German central government, but would reach no accord on four-power measures to effect German economic and political unity, which the Western powers deemed prerequisite to the establishment of a central government.[43] In February, 1948, then, the United States, the United Kingdom, and France were to open in London what they described as "informal discussions of German problems," to which the Benelux countries were invited to send representatives. The London Six-Power Conference which ended in June, 1948, had as its purpose to recommend measures for the integration of the economic and political life of Western Germany into that of western Europe, in the absence of agreement between the four occupying powers on economic and political implementation for Germany as a whole.[44]

Even as the London Six-Power Conference was in progress, and before its recommendations were published, the U.S.S.R. sent notes of protest to the Western powers that the convening of the conference constituted a violation of existing four-power agreements, for the conference was to consider matters within the competence of the Council of Foreign Ministers and the Control Council in Germany, matters not to be decided otherwise than by agreement among all the four powers occupying Germany.[45] The West replied that discussions contemplating the establishment of a West German government in no way precluded ultimate four-power agree-

9

ment on the future of Germany as a whole.[46] But this Western rejection of Soviet protests was followed on March 20, 1948 by the Soviet military governor's withdrawal from the Control Council.[47] The Control Council did not meet again on a quadripartite basis.[48]

On March 30, 1948 the Soviet Military Administration in East Germany informed the three Western military governors of the imposition of a series of restrictions on rail and highway traffic between the Western zones and Berlin through the Soviet zone, purportedly justified as border and customs control measures. Later, more stringent, restrictions were explained as necessitated by "technical difficulties."[49] By June 24, 1948 all land and water traffic to and from the western sectors of Berlin had been halted by Soviet zone authorities; only the Western airlift, over which Soviet authorities could exert no effective control short of armed attack, linked West Berlin with the West. This total blockade was said by the Soviet military governor to have been compelled, in protection of the interests of the German population of Berlin and the Soviet zone, by the currency reform measures introduced in Western Germany and extended to West Berlin on June 24, 1948.[50] When representatives of the Western occupying powers met with Stalin and Molotov in August, 1948, to attempt to have the blockade lifted, it appeared that the purpose of the blockade was to force suspension of Western plans for the establishment of a West German government.[51] Whatever these reasons, many Western observers believed the blockade to have been undertaken by the U.S.S.R. as economic and political coercion designed to bring to an end Western occupation of Berlin, thus to close a loophole in the European iron curtain and to ensure that Soviet political and economic measures in East Germany could be carried out in relative secrecy. At the same time the influence of the political parties of the Western zones could be eliminated from the Soviet zone.[52] But one commentator points out of the state of affairs in East Germany in 1948:

In spite of the difficulties created by the loophole in the iron curtain, Soviet economic exploitation had not been hampered, or modified, by one jot. Though the lack of popular support for the SED [Socialist Unity Party, the Soviet zone fusion of Communist and Social Democratic parties] was patent, open Soviet support

10

had nevertheless clamped the Unity Party on the administrative and political life of the zone.[53]

He suggests rather that the U.S.S.R. even then intended the evacuation of Western troops from Berlin to be but prelude to a plan for a reunited Communist Germany under Soviet domination, which the U.S.S.R. was ready immediately to implement.[54]

Whatever the political considerations which motivated the Soviet blockade of Berlin in 1948, the ostensible issue was currency reform, and the Soviets were to use it to assert that there was no longer a legal basis for Western presence in Berlin nor concomitant rights of unrestricted access thereto for military or commercial traffic. Currency reform for Germany as a whole had been discussed in the Control Council for more than a year without quadripartite agreement on a plan.[55] The Control Council in suspense after the Soviet military governor's withdrawal in March, the Western military governors proceeded on June 18, 1948 to issue a currency reform law for their own zones, but the reform was not to extend to Berlin as the city was under quadripartite control still.[56] The Soviet military governor's response was to denounce the tripartite action as a violation of agreements that German financial matters were to be decided upon by the four powers jointly, to assert that Greater Berlin was territorially and economically part of the Soviet zone of occupation, and to claim that henceforth only the Soviet Military Administration, and not the Allied *Komendatura*, had the right to enact currency reform legislation for the whole of Berlin.[57] On June 22, 1948 Soviet authorities issued orders for a separate currency reform for their zone and all of Berlin.[58] The three Western military governors immediately informed the Soviet military governor that a new currency linked to the West German currency would be introduced into their sectors in Berlin, and this was done on June 25, 1948.[59] The Soviet blockade of land and water traffic to and from Berlin was then total. Western counter-blockade measures began gradually to be instituted, and by September 13, 1948 interzonal land traffic was at a standstill.[60]

Governmental discussions between representatives of the four powers with respect to the Berlin blockade took place without result in Moscow and Berlin until early in September, 1948.[61] The Berlin blockade was then referred to the United Nations Security Council by the Western powers as "a threat to peace" under Chapter VII of the United Nations Charter, still without achievement of a solution.[62] Through these negotiations the West insisted that the successive Soviet interferences with land and water traffic between Berlin and the Western zones were unwarranted violations of express and implied agreements between the powers establishing Western rights of unrestricted access to Berlin, which rights had been confirmed in three years' working practice. The Western case for freedom of movement to and from Berlin for their occupying forces was strong. The Protocol of September 12, 1944 establishing Berlin as a special area of joint occupation surrounded by the Soviet zone of occupation implied a right of way through the Soviet zone for the transit and provisioning of Western occupying troops in Berlin. This understanding was specified in the exchange of messages between Truman, Churchill, and Stalin on June 14-18, 1945, and confirmed by the express agreement of Marshal Zhukov and Generals Clay and Weeks on June 29, 1945 on details of the orderly exercise of Western rights of passage. These details were amplified in later actions of the Allied control authority in Germany. The Western case for a right of access to Berlin for freight traffic from the West under commercial auspices, and over routes other than those specifically designated for the use of Western military garrisons in Berlin, was almost as strong. Wartime planning in the European Advisory Commission had proceeded on the assumption that Germany would be treated as a political and economic unit and therefore no special provisions would be needed to regulate the economic relations between Berlin and any of the zones.[63] These too were the principles agreed upon at Potsdam. But the Western powers were able to point specifically to the July 7, 1945 agreement of their military representatives to the Soviet request that they assume responsibility for the physical well-being of civilians in the western sectors of Berlin. This obligation, undertaken at Soviet insistence, involved import of food and fuel to Berlin from the Western zones and abroad, and necessarily implied that there was to be freedom of movement through the Soviet zone to West Berlin for commercial freight traffic from the West. Such traffic over all routes to Berlin had become established in practice over three years, and its halt at the order of Soviet authorities was an illegal interference with the proper discharge of Western responsibilities to ensure the provisioning of the civilian inhabitants of the western sectors of Berlin.[64] However freedom of access to Berlin from the West for civilian passenger traffic would appear, in the case of Germans, to have been conditioned upon compliance with interzonal pass requirements established by the Control Council. But even civilians with valid travel authorization could not move to or from Berlin by land when all transportation through the Soviet zone was ordered to a halt. What legal justification the U.S.S.R. offered for its blockade of Berlin was based on its assertion that Berlin was part of the Soviet zone and that Soviet occupying authorities alone had the right to control affairs in Berlin and in the Soviet zone, the Western powers having forfeited their right to participate in the occupation and administration of Berlin and joint control of Germany as a whole by alleged violations of reparations agreements, the creation of Bizonia, and the introduction of a separate currency reform for the Western zones of Germany.

By the spring of 1949 it was becoming clear to the Soviet Union that the West would continue the Berlin airlift indefinitely rather than abandon West Berlin, and that the interzonal trade embargo was having a more serious impact on East Germany than on Western Germany.[65] On May 4, 1949 the four powers agreed to lift all restrictions any of them had imposed since March 1, 1948 on communications, transportation, and trade between Berlin and their zones and between the Eastern and Western zones.[66] The meeting of the Council of Foreign Ministers in Paris in May and June, 1949, was to be the final, unsuccessful attempt of the four powers to reach an agreement for the resumption of quadripartite government of Germany as a whole. With respect to Berlin, the four foreign ministers recorded their common view that the agreement of May 4, 1949 was to be maintained.[67]

The Berlin *Komendatura* had continued to meet even after the Control Council had ceased to function, but on June 16, 1948, the eve of total blockade, the Soviet commandant withdrew from a meeting of the *Komendatura* and refused to rejoin that authority.[68] In the course of the Berlin blockade there were established in the Soviet sector a separate City Assembly, Magistrat, and municipal administrative agencies rivalling those already existing for the city as a whole, purporting to be the only legal organs of the city government but restricted in effective action to the Soviet sector.[69] When the Berlin blockade ended in May, 1949, quadripartite control of the city was also at an end in fact. The eastern and western sectors were separately administered thereafter, but until 1961 there was relative freedom of movement between sectors within the city.

C. *The Present Division of Germany*

Military government ended in Western Germany, but not an occupation régime, with the establishment of a West German Government, the Federal Republic of Germany,[70] and the entry into operation on September 21, 1949 of the Occupation Statute[71] and the Charter of the Allied High Commission, to which an Agreement on Tripartite Controls is annexed.[72] The United States, the United Kingdom, and France, declaring that they retained the supreme authority in Germany assumed by them under the Declaration of June 5, 1945,[73] established an Allied High Commission for the exercise of supreme Allied authority in the Federal Republic of Germany.[74] All authority of the Western military governors with respect to the control of Germany was transferred to the three High Commissioners, who were to exercise that authority in accordance with the Charter of the Commission and the Occupation Statute. The Occupation Statute defined the division of powers between the Allied High Commission and the German authorities in the Federal Republic with regard to the government of West Germany. The German people were intended to enjoy self-government to the maximum possible degree consistent with a continuing occupation régime; hence the Federal State and the participating *Länder* were accorded by virtue of the Occupation Statute full legislative, executive, and judicial powers in accordance with the Basic Law of the Federal Republic and with the constitutions of the *Länder*, subject only to the limitations set out further in the Occupation Statute. The Statute then enumerated the fields in which powers were spe-

14

cifically reserved to the occupying authorities in order to ensure the accomplishment of the basic purposes of the occupation. The occupying authorites reserved as well the right, on instructions from their governments, "to resume, in whole or in part, the exercise of full authority if they consider that to do so is essential to security or to preserve democratic government in Germany or in pursuance of the international obligations of their governments."

On May 5, 1955, with the entry into operation of the revised Bonn Conventions,[75] the occupation régime in the Federal Republic of Germany ended and a new relationship with the United States, the United Kingdom, and France began. The Federal Republic was to have "the full authority of a sovereign State over its internal and external affairs,"[76] with certain important reservations. The three Western powers retain for an indefinite time rights theretofore exercised or held by them which relate to Berlin and to Germany as a whole, including the reunification of Germany and a peace settlement, and to the stationing of armed forces in Germany insofar as required for the exercise of these retained rights.[77] There entered into force as well on May 5, 1955 the accession of the Federal Republic of Germany to the North Atlantic Treaty;[78] within the framework of the North Atlantic Treaty Organization, West German rearmament was to be permitted. On September 14, 1955 the U.S.S.R. accorded full diplomatic recognition to the Federal Republic of Germany.[79]

Constitutional development in West Germany was formally paralleled in East Germany by the creation in October, 1949 of an East German government called the German Democratic Republic and possessing, as the Federal Republic did not then, a Ministry of Foreign Affairs.[80] The promulgation of the Constitution of the German Democratic Republic was not accompanied by the publication of any instrument defining the relationship between the East German government and the occupying forces of the Soviet Union. On October 10, 1949 the Soviet Military Administration turned itself into a Soviet Control Commission of roughly similar construction.[81]

On September 20, 1955, several months after the termination of the Western occupation régime in the Federal Republic, a treaty

15

was signed between the U.S.S.R. and the German Democratic Republic in which the parties confirmed "that the relations between them are based on complete equality of rights, mutual respect of sovereignty and the non-interference in domestic affairs," "taking into consideration the obligations of the GDR and the Soviet Union under the international agreements which concern Germany as a whole."[82] However the Soviet troops stationed on the territory of the German Democratic Republic "in accordance with the existing international agreements" were to remain there temporarily with the approval of the East German government. The treaty was accompanied by an exchange of letters which declared that the German Democratic Republic was to exercise control over East German borders with the Federal Republic of Germany and with West Berlin, and over lines of communication between the Federal Republic and West Berlin, except with respect to the movement of Western military personnel and matériel to West Berlin, control over which would continue "temporarily [to] be exercised by the command of Soviet troops in Germany, pending conclusion of an appropriate agreement."[83] The exchange of letters further stated:

> In the control and guarding of lines of communication between the German Federal Republic and West Berlin situated on GDR territory, the GDR will insure with the appropriate authorities of the German Federal Republic, the settlement of all matters connected with rail and road traffic and the passage of shipping of the German Federal Republic and West Berlin, their citizens or inhabitants and foreign states and their citizens, except for the personnel and material of the troops of the United States, Great Britain, and France in West Berlin. . . .

On September 20, 1955 there was issued as well a Soviet statement announcing the dissolution of the Soviet Control Commission in Germany.[84] The Soviet Ambassador to the German Democratic Republic would maintain with the representatives of the three Western powers in the Federal Republic of Germany relations pertaining to matters arising from decisions of the four powers on all-German questions. The statement went on to declare that laws issued by the Control Council in exercise of the occupation rights

16

of the four powers were deprived of effect in the territory of the German Democratic Republic, but added:

> The abolition of these Control Council regulations in the territory of the German Democratic Republic does not affect the rights and obligations of the Soviet Union regarding the whole of Germany which arise from the relevant decisions of the four Powers.

The German Democratic Republic has acceded to the Warsaw Security Treaty,[85] and maintains diplomatic relations with the members of that Pact. The Western powers have refused to recognize the sovereignty of the German Democratic Republic. They maintain that the government of the Federal Republic of Germany is the only German government freely and legitimately constituted, hence the only representative of the German people entitled to speak for Germany pending eventual reunification.[86]

The lifting of the Berlin blockade in 1949 had not signalled complete Soviet acquiescence in Western assertions that access to Berlin was of right to be unrestricted. Soviet authorities continued sporadically to interfere with non-military traffic between Berlin and the Western zones, though each new set of restrictions was short-lived; the Western powers would lodge formal protests and sometimes institute retaliatory measures.[87] But with the establishment of West German and East German governments a new disagreement arose between the U.S.S.R. and the Western powers over continuing Soviet responsibility for supervision and control of Western access to Berlin. On January 27, 1950 the East German Ministry of the Interior had announced that thenceforth all Western traffic into or through the Soviet zone of Germany or the Soviet sector of Berlin would be required to obtain special permits from the East German People's Police. Soviet authorities on February 1, 1950 transferred supervision of East-West boundaries in Germany to the East German People's Police.[88] Thereafter Soviet authorities were increasingly to respond to Western notes on civilian access to Berlin that these were matters within the sole competence of authorities of the German Democratic Republic.[89] Stiffest Western protest was delivered upon the announcement of the September 20, 1955 treaty between the U.S.S.R. and the German Democratic Republic and its accompanying instruments. In notes to the Soviet Union the Western governments declared that these U.S.S.R.-G.D.R. agreements could not affect in any way the obligations or responsibilities of the U.S.S.R. under agreements and arrangements on the subject of Germany, including Berlin, previously concluded between the Soviet Union and the Western powers.

> The three governments consider that the U.S.S.R. remains bound by the engagements which it has assumed vis-à-vis the Three Powers concerning Germany, and that, in particular, the letters exchanged between Mr. Zorin and Mr. Bolz on the 20th of September 1955 cannot have the effect of discharging the U.S.S.R. from the responsibilities which it has assumed in matters concerning transportation and communications between the different parts of Germany, including Berlin.[90]

To this day none of the Western occupying powers nor the Federal Republic of Germany has recognized the German Democratic Republic as a legitimately constituted or sovereign government. Yet in matters concerned with trade and civilian traffic between the West and Berlin over land routes through East Germany — passport and customs control, rail, water, and road transport — there is constant contact between West German and East German officials; perhaps ninety-five per cent of all civilian traffic between the Federal Republic of Germany and West Berlin is so arranged.[91] The Bonn government maintains that these are "technical contacts" at the governmental level of experts and subordinate officials, without political meaning, and do not involve recognition of East German pretensions to sovereignty. The Western powers appear to take the position that these dealings with "minor functionaries of the so-called GDR" in no way imply Western acceptance of the East German régime as a substitute for the U.S.S.R. in the discharge of obligations of the Soviet Union towards the West with regard to normal access to Berlin.[92] Soviet, and not East German, authorities continue to supervise Western military traffic along land access routes to Berlin through East Germany.[93]

18

D. *The Status of Berlin*

In the wartime planning of the four powers, Berlin was to be a single city occupied and administered by them jointly. The quadripartite *Komendatura* in Berlin functioned fairly smoothly until October, 1946, when elections were held throughout Greater Berlin. A non-Communist majority was established in the City Assembly, and it turned out of office most of the Soviet-appointed members of the executive Magistrat. Thereafter the work of the *Komendatura* was increasingly hampered by the Soviet commandant's use of the veto.[94] On June 16, 1948 the Soviet commandant withdrew from a meeting of the *Komendatura* and did not attend further meetings of the Western commandants. On July 1, 1948 the Soviet chief of staff in the *Komendatura* Secretariat stated formally that Soviet representatives would no longer participate in meetings of bodies of the *Komendatura*.[95]

On December 21, 1948 the three Western commandants in Berlin declared that the *Komendatura*, having been established by agreements which could be altered or abrogated only by agreement of all the governments party, had not ceased to exist, although its work had been in suspense since the Soviet commandant's refusal to attend its meetings. The Western commandants planned therefore to resume exercise of the powers of the *Komendatura*, although it might only be possible for them to carry out its decisions in the western sectors of Berlin. The Soviet commandant was free to return at any time to the *Komendatura*, they said, whereupon quadripartite rule of Berlin could be resumed.[96] The Western commandants have exercised the powers of the *Komendatura* on this basis ever since. The Allied Kommandatura functions as a quadripartite agency *de jure*, but a tripartite agency *de facto*, issuing orders to a city government which claims jurisdiction over all of Berlin but which operates in fact only in the three western sectors.

West Berlin could not remain unaffected by the establishment of the new occupation régime in West Germany in 1949, but as the Western powers had insisted that Berlin could not be treated as part of the Soviet zone, neither could they jeopardize the quadripartite status of the city by treating its western sectors as part of the Western zones. The Occupation Statute for West Germany did

19

not apply to the western sectors of Berlin, but an instrument closely modelling it was drawn for Berlin by the Allied Kommandatura.
The May 14, 1949 Statement of Principles Governing the Relationship between the Allied Kommandatura and Greater Berlin,[97]
like the Occupation Statute, permitted a large measure of self-government, but specifically reserved to the Allied Kommandatura powers in certain fields and also the right to resume in whole
or in part the exercise of full authority "if they consider that to do
so is essential to security or to preserve democratic government,
or in pursuance of the international obligations of their Governments." The Kommandatura Statement of Principles provided in
addition:

> [I]n the special circumstances prevailing in Berlin, the Occupa-
> tion Authorities reserve the right to intervene, in an emergency,
> and issue orders to ensure the security, good order and financial
> and economic stability of the City.

An Agreement on a Revised Internal Procedure for the Allied
(Western) Kommandatura was also drawn which, like the Charter
of the Allied High Commission, *mutatis mutandis*, permits the
Kommandatura to take action upon majority vote, though approval of amendments to the city constitution requires unanimous
agreement.[98]

When the Federal Republic of Germany assumed a new status vis-
à-vis the Western powers in 1955, the occupation régime, somewhat
altered, was to continue in Berlin. On May 5, 1955 there came into
operation the Declaration by the Allied (Western) Kommandatura,[99] which was to grant to Berlin authorities "the maximum liberty compatible with the special situation of Berlin." Article II of
the Declaration recites:

> The Allied authorities retain the right to take, if they deem it
> necessary, such measures as may be required to fulfil their inter-
> national obligations, to ensure public order, and to maintain the
> status and security of Berlin and its economy, trade, and commu-
> nications.

Article III enumerates the fields in which the Allied authorities in

Berlin will normally exercise powers: security, interests and immunities of the Allied forces; disarmament and demilitarization; relations of Berlin with authorities abroad; satisfaction of occupation costs; and authority over the Berlin police to the extent necessary to ensure the security of Berlin.

So far as relations between Berlin and the Federal Republic of Germany are concerned, here too the Western powers have taken care to preserve the theoretical quadripartite status of the city. They have not thus far permitted the incorporation of West Berlin into the Federal Republic as a separate constituent *Land*.[100] The Basic Law of the Federal Republic does not now apply in West Berlin.[101] The city does not participate in Federal elections; Berlin may send delegates to the West German Bundestag, but only in an advisory non-voting capacity.[102] The provisions of any Federal law are to apply in Berlin only after they have been voted upon by the Berlin House of Representatives and passed as Berlin law.[103] However the economies of West Berlin and the Federal Republic are integrated,[104] and in two respects the assimilation of West Berlin to a *Land* of the Federal Republic has been permitted: it has been incorporated into the system of Federal finance administration, so that revenues and expenditures are regulated between the Federal Republic and West Berlin as they are between the Federal Republic and the West German *Länder*;[105] and the jurisdiction of all Federal supreme courts but the Federal Constitutional Court extends to Berlin.[106]

Concerning the *renversement* which has occurred in Germany in the last sixteen years, East and West are in accord on one point: that the situation of Berlin is "abnormal." The fortunes of war and diplomacy have left the people of West Berlin 110 miles behind the Iron Curtain, but the Western powers are now solemnly committed to preserve West Berlin from absorption by their wartime ally, the Soviet Union. Western military presence in Berlin, originally intended to serve the security of the occupying powers against the German people, now sustains the opportunity for more than two million West Berliners to determine their own future and way of life. All the other Parties to the North Atlantic Treaty have associated themselves with the repeated declarations of the United States, the

21

United Kingdom, and France that they will treat any attack against Berlin from any quarter as an attack upon their forces and themselves.[107] It is, however, the positive aim of the West to end the confrontation in Berlin of Soviet and Western military force by four-power agreement on a peace treaty with Germany which would establish a reunited Berlin as the capital of a reunited Germany on the basis of free elections.[108] To conserve the legal basis for the reunification of Berlin, the Western occupying powers have made efforts to maintain the quadripartite status of Greater Berlin as an area of joint occupation and administration. They have insisted and continue formally to insist that, as agreed on July 7, 1945, transportation and movement within Berlin are to be unrestricted between the sectors, for Germans as well as for Western military personnel and civilian officials of the Berlin command, and that it is the responsibility of the Soviet military command in Berlin to ensure this free movement in the eastern sector.[109]

The Soviet Union does even now acquiesce in the maintenance of an occupation régime in West Berlin, and one vestige of the Western right to unrestricted movement within Greater Berlin is still observed: Soviet military authorities raise the barrier at the one access point to East Berlin which is open to foreigners, to permit entry of United States, British, and French military vehicles carrying uniformed soldiers on motor patrols within the eastern sector about twelve times a day.[110] But in the eastern sector of Berlin a separate city administration has been established since 1948 which claims to be the legal government of Greater Berlin, and which has been recognized as such by Soviet authorities.[111] In Article 2 of the Constitution of the German Democratic Republic, Berlin is declared to be its capital, and in East Berlin are installed the President and all major government departments of East Germany. At present (January 12, 1962) Greater Berlin is physically divided by an East German-erected wall of concrete and barbed wire through which there is but one entry from West Berlin to East Berlin for foreigners, at the Friedrichstrasse in the American sector. All persons other than uniformed Western military personnel are there halted by East German police, and must produce satisfactory documents and undergo customs inspection before they are allowed to enter the eastern sector.[112] The Soviet Union was slow to permit the absorption of East Berlin into the German Democratic Republic,[113] which led the Western powers to think there might yet be Russian agreement to reunification of Greater Berlin under quadripartite rule. But the only reunification of the divided city which the U.S.S.R. apparently contemplates "would be for the western part of Berlin, now actually detached from the GDR, to be reunited with its eastern part and for Berlin to become a unified city within the state in whose territory it is situated."[114] It has become clear that when the Soviet Union speaks of "the quadripartite status of Berlin," it now refers only to the status of West Berlin. The current Berlin crisis was precipitated by Soviet proposals in November, 1958 to alter the status of West Berlin.

II. Contentions of The Powers Concerning Western Legal Rights in Berlin

A. *The Soviet "Free City of West Berlin" Proposal*

On November 27, 1958 notes from the Soviet Union were given to the Ambassadors at Moscow of the United States,[115] the United Kingdom, France, and the Federal Republic of Germany which stated that the U.S.S.R. could no longer tolerate the continued existence of an occupation régime in West Berlin being used by the West "as a vantage point from which to carry on hostile activities against the socialist countries." The Western powers were notified that the Soviet Union regarded "as null and void" the 1944 and 1945 agreements under which arrangements had been made between the victors for the occupation and control of defeated Germany. The U.S.S.R. announced that it planned "at an appropriate time" to turn over to the German Democratic Republic all Soviet occupation functions in East Germany, including control over the West's access routes to West Berlin. "It is envisaged that the German Democratic Republic, like any other independent state, must fully deal with questions concerning its space, i.e., exercise its sovereignty on land, on water, and in the air." For a time, however, the Soviet Union would make no changes in existing procedures respecting the movement of Western military traffic to and from West Berlin, if in that time the interested countries were to arrange such a liquidation of the occupation régime in West Berlin as the U.S.S.R. then proposed: that the four wartime allies agree with the German Democratic Republic to convert West Berlin into a free city, completely demilitarized and with its own government, independent of both East and West Germany, the four powers to arrange with the German Democratic Republic for guarantees of unhindered communications between the free city and the outside world with the object of free movement of passenger and freight traffic, West Berlin in its turn to undertake not to permit on its territory "any hostile subversive activity directed against the GDR or any other state."

24

The Western powers were to reply that the proposal for a "so-called 'free city' " as put forward by the Soviet Union was unacceptable.[116] Neither would they accept a unilateral denunciation by the U.S.S.R. of its obligations under existing agreements with the United States, the United Kingdom, and France with respect to their presence in Berlin and freedom of access to the city, nor agree to the substitution of German authorities of the Soviet zone for the Soviet government insofar as those obligations are concerned. The Western governments affirmed their determination to maintain their position and their rights with respect to Berlin, including the right of free access.

B. *Supporting Arguments of the Soviet Union*

The Soviet Union maintains that, in light of developments in Germany since 1945, the Western powers no longer have any right to occupy any part of Berlin, and that the U.S.S.R. is no longer obliged to protect or even to tolerate a special status for Berlin, Western presence there, or Western rights of access thereto. What international engagements with the Western powers may bind it to such obligations, the U.S.S.R. repudiates. Such repudiation is justified, it asserts, because: (1) the Western powers have on their part grossly violated those agreements; (2) the West has abused its rights under those agreements, using its position in West Berlin to direct subversive activities against the Soviet Union; (3) the agreements have by their terms expired; and (4) the agreements are in any case obsolete in view of changed circumstances in Germany. The supporting arguments of the Soviet Union require that the September 12, 1944 Protocol on Zones of Occupation and Administration of Greater Berlin, the November 14, 1944 Agreement on Control Machinery in Germany, and the Potsdam Protocol of August 1, 1945 be considered as interdependent agreements. These arguments run:

(1) Greater Berlin has always been part of the Soviet zone; however by Allied agreement it was given a special status for the particular purposes of the Allied occupation of Germany. As Berlin had been the capital of Germany, and would undoubtedly be the

25

capital of the united, democratic, and peace-loving Germany which the victorious powers envisioned for the future, it was chosen as the natural seat for the Allied authority which was in the interim and to these ends to exercise supreme authority jointly in matters affecting Germany as a whole. Hence by the Protocol of September 12, 1944 the Allies established three (later, four) zones of occupation in Germany, but not a specific fifth zone comprising the territory of Greater Berlin; rather, Berlin was only to be subject to joint Allied administration and occupation, without its territorial integrity with the eastern zone being affected. Proponents of this argument[117] point to language in the November 14, 1944 Agreement on Control Machinery in Germany which provides that: "Supreme authority in Germany will be exercised ... by the Commanders-in-Chief ... , each in his own zone of occupation, and also jointly, in matters affecting Germany as a whole, in their capacity as members of the ... [Control Council]," but mentions Berlin only to recite that a *Komendatura* will be established "to direct jointly the administration of the 'Greater Berlin' area." They interpret this language to mean that only the Soviet commander-in-chief was to exercise supreme authority in Greater Berlin, save as supreme authority was to be exercised jointly in matters affecting Germany as a whole; the Western powers were to enjoy only the right of co-management in the occupation and administration of Berlin.

(2) Actions of the Western powers inconsistent with the Potsdam principles which were to govern Allied treatment of defeated Germany have brought to an end Allied arrangements for the quadripartite exercise of supreme authority in Germany. The Control Council having ceased to exist thirteen years ago, there is no longer reason to accord a special status to Berlin. Nor is there any longer an obligation incumbent upon the Soviet Union to tolerate continued Western presence in Berlin which would perpetuate that status. The Western powers are themselves accused of violating Allied agreements to which they would hold the Soviet Union. As well as its grievances about reparations, Bizonia, and separate currency reform, the U.S.S.R. now complains of the creation of a separate State

26

in West Germany, the rearmament of that State, and its inclusion in a defense alliance hostile to the Soviet Union. To these reasons to justify Soviet denunciation of Allied agreements it adds the justification of self-preservation:[118] the West uses its position in Berlin to threaten the security of the Soviet Union.

(3) As Allied arrangements for the quadripartite exercise of supreme authority in Germany have terminated, and the Western powers have forfeited their right to participate in the co-management of Berlin, there is no longer any limitation on the supreme authority of the Soviet Union in the Soviet zone of occupation, Greater Berlin included within that territory. The U.S.S.R. has thus been able to grant full independence to the territory of East Germany, as the Western powers have to West Germany. Hence there exist on the territory of pre-1938 Germany two fully sovereign States, to both of which the Soviet Union has accorded formal diplomatic recognition. What rights with respect to Berlin and access thereto the U.S.S.R. may have retained, it can relinquish to the German Democratic Republic in a separate peace treaty; there no longer exists any requirement that the Western powers join in the grant. After that, continued Western occupation of West Berlin and transit thereto across East Germany would be incongruous with the territorial sovereignty of the German Democratic Republic. Unless the Western powers were to make new arrangements with the German Democratic Republic, the continuance of a Western occupation régime in West Berlin could only be interpreted by the members of the Warsaw Security Pact as an act of aggression against one of their number, which will cause appropriate retaliation. For the sake of strengthening peace in Europe, however, the German Democratic Republic will as a gracious concession agree to the conversion of West Berlin into such a demilitarized free city as the Soviet Union proposes.

C. Legal Contentions of the Western Powers

The Western powers deny that Berlin is now or ever was part of the Soviet zone of occupation. The September 12, 1944 Protocol clearly establishes Greater Berlin as a special area of joint occu-

27

pation apart from the zonal divisions of Germany. The territorial arrangements it provided for were put into effect in July, 1945 with the withdrawal of American and British troops from parts of the prescribed Soviet zone and the movement of troops of the Western powers to Berlin. The Soviet Union having derived its full advantage from that agreement can not now deprive the Western powers of their compensating advantages nor prevent them from fulfilling corresponding responsibilities for their sectors of occupation in Berlin. At Soviet insistence Berlin has from the beginning of the occupation been a separate economic area in Germany as well, the Western occupying powers having undertaken to be responsible for the maintenance of the civilian population of their sectors.

The West insists further that the continuance of its occupation of Berlin, which derives from rights of conquest and the Protocol of September 12, 1944, does not at all depend on other Allied agreements concerning the control and treatment of Germany. The Agreement on Control Machinery of November 14, 1944 by its terms contemplates that new arrangements will be made between the four powers for the control of Germany after it will have fulfilled the basic requirements of unconditional surrender; the Protocol of September 12, 1944 is not so limited with respect to duration. Neither do Western rights derived from conquest and the Protocol of September 12, 1944 depend for their continued validity upon implementation of the principles of the Potsdam Protocol, concluded later in time and concerned with a different subject. Moreover, it is the Soviet Union that bears responsibility for the fact that the Potsdam agreement could not be implemented.

The Western powers maintain that they have done nothing in Germany which implies repudiation of quadripartite control of Germany as a whole; in fact the possibility of a resumption of quadripartite control and reunification of Germany has been carefully preserved in arrangements they have made with the Federal Republic of Germany.[119] They have as well done everything in their power to conserve the quadripartite status of Berlin. They refuse to acquiesce in the unilateral Soviet repudiation of these international agreements.

The West contends that there are not two Germanies; the government of the Federal Republic is the only German government freely and legitimately constituted, hence the only representative of the German people entitled to speak for Germany in international affairs. The Soviet Union may make what arrangements it will with the territory which it actually occupies, but no separate peace treaty between it and East Germany can cut off Western rights vis-à-vis East Germany with respect to Berlin and access thereto, for the four powers assumed supreme authority in Germany jointly on June 5, 1945, and that joint supreme authority persists. Were that authority to expire it must be by mutual consent; the Western powers have not by words or conduct indicated acquiescence in an end to the authority, and they point out that the U.S.S.R. itself has taken action and entered into agreements inconsistent with belief that joint supreme authority with respect to Germany as a whole has terminated.[120] Therefore the Western powers continue to hold the U.S.S.R. responsible for the Eastern zone of Germany and the eastern sector of Berlin. They have repeatedly declared their willingness to consider with the Soviet Union any arrangement or treaty in Germany consistent with the maintenance of peace and freedom and with the legitimate security interests of all nations. But until a satisfactory peace settlement has been concluded with Germany as a whole, or they agree otherwise, the Western powers claim the right to continue in occupation of their sectors in Berlin, to exercise supreme authority there, and to have unrestricted access thereto in accordance with existing international agreements which the Soviet Union is bound to observe.

The Forum: A Summary of the Proceedings

1. Background of the Berlin-German Crisis*

Professor BOWIE introduced the subject by stating that the problem in Berlin is how to apply the rights and obligations growing out of the conquest of Germany and the 1944 and 1945 agreements of the four victorious powers to the conditions which exist in Germany today. The premise upon which those agreements were concluded was that Germany would be governed and would function as a single unit. Accordingly, supreme authority over Germany was assumed by the four powers jointly upon unconditional surrender, and control machinery was established for the joint exercise by all four of that supreme authority.

For the purposes of occupation, Germany was to be divided into four zones, one to be allotted to each power, plus a special Berlin area, which was to be under joint occupation and administration. "Apparently the Western powers expected that the Soviet Union would in good faith cooperate in working the control machinery in Germany so as to attain the purposes which were broadly stated in the Potsdam agreement. For its part, the Soviet Union must have believed initially that the Communists in Germany were strong enough to exploit the social and economic chaos and the political vacuum there at the end of the war so as to take control fairly rapidly, as indeed happened in other parts of eastern Europe."

But it became manifest in the first year of the occupation, Professor BOWIE pointed out, that the expectations of both sides were to be disappointed. The Western powers soon realized that the Soviet Union did not intend to join in carrying out the policies of the Potsdam Protocol, nor in operating the control machinery to achieve these aims. The Soviet Union discovered, he supposed,

*Except for direct quotations, which are so indicated, the discussion which took place at the forum is condensed, and therefore paraphrased. The condensation was prepared by Miss Doris Carroll, Research Assistant at the Harvard Law School.

when Berlin elections were held in 1946 and the Communists gained very few votes, that despite chaotic conditions in Germany the Communist Party would certainly not be able to take over in the Western zones nor even in the western sectors of Berlin. The eventual result of these disillusions was the breakdown of quadripartite control in Germany, and, by 1947, the existence of a very serious dilemma for the Western powers: unless they acted together at least with respect to their own zones, Soviet obstructionism which prevented treatment of Germany as an economic entity would lead at length to political disorder and economic collapse in the heart of Europe. Thus compelled, the United States and the United Kingdom first brought about an economic fusion of their zones. When, in 1948, the three Western powers proposed to grant a measure of self-government to Western Germany, and to ally the economic and political life of the democratic régime with that of western Europe, the Soviet Union began a total land blockade of isolated Berlin. The blockade failed of its purpose. The West instituted the Berlin airlift, and flew in supplies to the beleaguered city for more than a year rather than abandon it or suspend plans for the establishment of the Federal Republic of Germany.

The Federal Republic of Germany has since taken its place in the western European community, Professor BOWIE continued, joining the Coal and Steel Community in 1952, and becoming a member of NATO in 1954. For its part, the U.S.S.R. has created in the Soviet zone a satellite regime under one-party Communist control, called the German Democratic Republic, which has joined the Warsaw Pact alliance. More than one hundred miles inside the borders of Soviet-controlled East Germany is the divided city of Berlin, its western sectors still under Western occupation. West Berlin's economic and political life is closely tied to that of the Federal Republic; and the Western powers are solemnly committed to preserve West Berlin from absorption into the Soviet bloc. The current Berlin crisis was precipitated by Soviet proposals in 1958 to alter the status of West Berlin.

2. Legal Issues in the Berlin Dispute

Professor BOWIE centered his discussion of the legal aspects of the Berlin crisis around the Soviet note of November 27, 1958, which proposed that West Berlin be converted into a demilitarized "free city", the East German régime to guarantee free access to the city, and West Berlin to be committed to prevent subversive activities there directed against the Soviet bloc. In that note the U.S.S.R. asserted that Western violations of 1944 and 1945 agreements with the Soviet Union concerning the control of Germany, and especially of the Potsdam agreement, and subversive activities of the Western countries carried on in West Berlin, had undermined the legal basis for Western rights in the city and had released the Soviet Union from its obligations. The note said further that if the West did not agree to the proposed alteration of the status of West Berlin, the Soviet Union would cease to assure Western access to the city. It would transfer its occupation obligations to the East German régime and support that régime in the exercise of sovereignty on land, water, and in the air — in particular, its control of access routes to Berlin.

In reply to the Soviet note, the Western governments affirmed their determination to remain in Berlin and to insist upon free access to the city, rights which are founded on the conquest of Germany, quadripartite assumption of supreme authority with respect to Germany in 1945, and four-power agreements concerning exercise of that supreme authority. They rejected any Soviet repudiation of its four-power obligations, and refused to agree to the substitution of German authorities of the Soviet zone for the Soviet government insofar as those obligations were concerned. Finally, the Western governments declared that the Soviet "free city" proposal was unacceptable. "Thus, in the exchange of notes, the legal issues in the Berlin dispute were clearly joined: the right of the Western powers to remain in Berlin; their rights of access to Berlin for military and civilian purposes; and the status of West Berlin."

a. The Right of the West to Remain in Berlin

Professor BOWIE and Mr. DEBEVOISE agreed that the right of the Western powers to occupy Berlin is derived primarily from the total defeat and unconditional surrender of Germany to the four powers jointly, and the supreme authority in respect of Ger-

many assumed by the victors jointly on June 5, 1945. Mr. DEBE-
VOISE pointed out that:

"The right to occupy any part of a territory which has uncondi-
tionally surrendered is fundamental in international law; from
this source is derived as well the right of the Russians to enter into
occupation of their zone in Germany and the eastern sector of
Berlin."

The Russians counter by asserting that occupation after conquest
is a temporary measure, no longer justified in light of changed
conditions in Germany, and that they can cut off Western occupation rights in Berlin by concluding a separate peace treaty with the
satellite state in East Germany.

The second basis for Western occupation of Berlin, Mr. DE-
BEVOISE continued, is the four-power agreement of September
12, 1944, which provides that Berlin is to be a special area of joint
occupation and administration. The Russians launch an oblique
attack upon this legal ground for Western presence in Berlin. They
assert that the Berlin area has always been a part of the territory
of the Soviet zone, ignoring the express language of the occupation agreement and the maps which accompany it, all of which
clearly indicate that Greater Berlin, while within the borders of the
Soviet zone, is not to be considered a part of it. The Soviets also
attempt to make the quadripartite agreements of 1944 and 1945
interdependent arrangements. They then assert that the Western
powers, in allowing the Federal Republic to be formed and armed
and to join NATO, have violated the Potsdam Protocol and the
agreement on control machinery, and have thereby forfeited their
right to occupy Berlin. But, Mr. DEBEVOISE emphasized, the
occupation protocol is in no sense dependent upon the later-con-
cluded arrangements for the exercise of supreme authority in Germany, even if the Russians could show that the breakdown of quadripartite control of Germany was not due to Soviet intransigence
and obstructionism.

As an additional argument for continued Western presence in
Berlin, Mr. DEBEVOISE recalled that in 1945, when Western
troops had penetrated deep into the territory which was to be the

Soviet zone and the Soviet army was in sole occupation of Berlin, Stalin, Truman, and Churchill agreed to the mutual redistribution of forces into their prescribed occupation zones in Germany and sectors of occupation in Berlin. Western troops having been withdrawn from parts of the Soviet zone pursuant to the agreement of the Heads of Government and in accord with the occupation protocol, the West has performed its part of those arrangements, and cannot now be deprived of its *quid pro quo* — occupation of the western sectors of Berlin.

b. Western rights of access to Berlin

Mr. DEBEVOISE went on to say that the right of the West to have unrestricted access to Berlin from the Federal Republic by air and land routes through East Germany is based legally upon implied and express four-power agreements and on sixteen years' custom and usage. He noted that the formal quadripartite agreements of 1944 and 1945 prepared by the European Advisory Commission contain no express provisions about access to Berlin. But, he said, inasmuch as the occupation protocol established Berlin as a special area of joint occupation set within the Soviet zone borders, Western rights of access thereto are necessarily implied, adverting to customary international law concerning enclaves.

In response to a question from the floor as to "Why were these access rights not made explicit in the agreements?" Mr. DEBEVOISE replied that several explanations have been offered, among them: (1) that occupation of such an area so clearly implies access to that area for the occupying forces that it was believed unnecessary to make the understanding express; (2) that John G. Winant, American representative to the E.A.C., who was pressing to have access rights incorporated in the agreements, was advised by the War Department that access to Berlin was a purely 'military matter' which would be taken care of 'at the military level' when the time came; and (3) that in view of the continuing destruction of German railroads and highways by bombing, it would be unwise in wartime to specify allocation of particular access routes lest they prove impassable without extensive and time-consuming repair. Mr. McCLOY then joined the discussion, saying that he considered it neither useful nor relevant to attempt now to fix responsibility for the omission. Long after the Soviets had attempted to repudiate our rights, he had talked informally regarding the matter with both General Eisenhower and General Clay. He gained the impression from them that relations between Western and Soviet military authorities in Germany in the early days of the occupation were proceeding so well with respect to occupation matters, including the *de facto* recognition of all access rights, that it was not thought wise to press for a more definite written understanding than then existed.

In any event, these implied rights of access to Berlin were made express, Mr. DEBEVOISE continued, in the Stalin-Truman-Churchill correspondence of June, 1945, and supplemented by agreements of the military commanders and in later actions taken by the Allied control authority in Germany. Access rights were exercised by the West without restriction until the 1948 blockade. The Soviet-Western agreement of 1949 in effect ratified pre-existing practice by lifting all restrictions which had been imposed during the blockade. Soviet recognition of Western rights of access to Berlin is further evidenced in the arrangements made by the U.S.S.R. with East Germany in 1955, when control of Western civilian traffic to Berlin was entrusted to East German authorities, while Soviet authorities retained control over Western military traffic. Even now, the West exercises rights of access through East Germany to Berlin, though not without harassment. Mr. DEBEVOISE concluded his summary of the legal basis for Western access rights by referring to the 1960 decision of the International Court of Justice on Portuguese rights of passage through Indian territory to the Portuguese enclaves: The case, he said, is authority for the proposition that Western rights of access to Berlin will persist even if the Soviet Union conclude a separate peace treaty with East Germany relinquishing what occupation rights it has retained.

This discussion led to a question from the floor as to whether "the understanding concerning Western access to Berlin was clearly broad enough to encompass civilian traffic as well as military personnel and matériel movement." Mr. SCHWARZ answered that:

"Originally, of course, access agreements dealt with movements of the Western occupying forces. Immediately upon Western occupation of Berlin, however, the Russians insisted that food and coal for the civilian population of the western sectors be supplied from the Western zones or abroad, rather than from normal sources of supply in the Soviet zone. This obligation, undertaken upon Soviet request, necessarily implied freedom of movement through the Soviet zone for commercial freight traffic from the West. It is clear, moreover, that as planning for the German occupation had proceeded on the assumption that Germany would be treated as a political and economic unit, zonal frontiers were not initially intended or used to restrict movement of Germans within Germany. Hence rights of access to Berlin for civilian freight and passenger traffic are based upon these express and implied agreements and on the day-in-day-out practice of sixteen years."

Dr. CONANT then referred to rights of access for German civilians as well as Western military personnel within Berlin itself — a matter particularly pertinent in light of the events of August, 1961, and after, when East German authorities built the Wall and cut down the number of crossing points between East and West Berlin from ninety to six, and then to three. He said:

"It has seemed to me that in taking these actions, the Soviets were violating our rights under express agreements and customary practice, and if I, as a layman, may press into this legal area, I would submit the following argument: In the summer of 1946 the four commandants in Berlin approved a document known as the Temporary Constitution of Greater Berlin, which became effective the day after city-wide elections scheduled for October 20, 1946 had taken place. Article 2 of that Constitution provides that:
    (1) The whole of the German citizens of Greater Berlin manifest their will through their elected representative bodies.
    (2) All citizens of Greater Berlin, within the framework of the law, are of equal status, regardless of race, sex, confession, and extent of property owned.
I would contend that those provisions, the existence under that Constitution of a city government of Greater Berlin for more than a year, and established practice from July, 1945 until August, 1961 which permitted free movement between sectors for all the inhabitants of Greater Berlin, establish rights of unrestricted circulation throughout the city for its whole population. The right

of Western military personnel to move freely between East and West Berlin is well-settled, so I won't go into the details here. Furthermore, in notes to the Russians the West has repeatedly insisted on the quadripartite status of all of Berlin. It seems to me that in unilaterally reducing the number of access points to East Berlin, Soviet authorities have fundamentally altered that quadripartite status.

"In my opinion, therefore, the West had good legal reason to protest recent restrictions on free movement between sectors in Berlin. Whether we should now attempt to tear down the Wall is clearly a political or even a military problem, on which I do not feel competent to pass judgment."

c. The Legal Status of West Berlin

Mr. DEBEVOISE, continuing his exposition of the legal issues in the Berlin dispute, dealt next with the Soviet contention that the quadripartite status of West Berlin can no longer be maintained because the city is part of the territory of a sovereign state, the German Democratic Republic, which is entitled to control its relations with other countries and their use of its territory. Absent Western agreement to their "free city" plan, therefore, the Russians propose to end the special status of West Berlin by turning over to the East German régime full sovereignty over its territory. The U.S.S.R. maintains that such a separate treaty will cut off Western rights in respect of Berlin and access thereto. The Western powers, on the other hand, contend that the Soviet Union cannot unilaterally terminate Western rights derived from unconditional surrender, assumption of supreme authority in respect of Germany by the four powers jointly, and quadripartite agreements. Mr. DEBEVOISE continued:

"We of the West have often declared our willingness to conclude a satisfactory peace settlement for Germany as a whole, but we want to negotiate that treaty with a government which has been freely chosen by all the people of Germany. We now recognize the government of the Federal Republic as the only freely and legitimately constituted government which exists in Germany; we refuse to recognize that the Soviet-controlled puppet government of East Germany is entitled to speak for those people in international affairs."

"But what, as a matter of international law, are the considerations which lead to the conclusion that the Federal Republic of Germany is 'legitimate' and the German Democratic Republic 'illegitimate'?", a member of the audience asked.

Professor BOWIE answered:

"As you know, the criteria for recognition of governments are by no means universally acknowledged. But one generally accepted criterion is the question whether the government is in effective control of the territory. It seems to me that even on this narrow ground it is possible to distinguish between the two governments. It is quite obvious that the government of the Federal Republic was freely elected by the people of West Germany, rules by their consent, and is, in fact, in effective control of its territory. If you examine the evidence, it is equally clear, I believe, that the government of East Germany has been imposed on the people there. I think that if Soviet forces were removed, the government would be overthrown in a matter of days or weeks. It seems to me, therefore, that even on this narrow ground it is perfectly proper to take the view that the East German government is not effectively in control of the territory, but that the Soviet Union is the actual government there, acting through agents or puppets like Ulbricht."

The Soviets claim, Mr. DEBEVOISE added, that the Western powers no longer have a voice in East German and Berlin affairs because in creating the Federal Republic they themselves brought joint supreme authority in Germany to an end. But in ending the occupation régime in West Germany, the Allies expressly retained rights theretofore exercised or held which relate to Berlin and to Germany as a whole, including the reunification of Germany and a peace settlement. Such action is inconsistent with an intention to renounce joint supreme authority. Moreover, the Western powers also took care to preserve the theoretical quadripartite status of Berlin when they granted a measure of self-government to the western sectors. For its part, the U.S.S.R., in its arrangements with the German Democratic Republic made in 1955, similarly reserved rights derived from the joint assumption of supreme authority; among other documents, the treaty recites that the parties are "taking into consideration the obligations of the GDR and the Soviet Union under the international agreements which concern Germany as a whole." This Soviet language, said Mr. DEBEVOISE, is inconsistent with Soviet belief in its assertions that the Western powers no longer have any rights in regard to Berlin and Germany as a whole which the U.S.S.R. must respect.

In his comments, Mr. SCHWARZ too adverted to the international legal consequences of a separately concluded peace treaty between the Soviet Union and the German Democratic Republic. "I have no doubt in my own mind," he said, "that law and world opinion would support our contention that such a treaty would in no way alter legitimate Western rights in Berlin. We cannot enjoin the conclusion of that treaty, if indeed its negotiation is anything more than a Russian threat, but it seems to me that it would not change our situation at all."

3. Political Implications of the Berlin Crisis

In his address, Professor BOWIE emphasized that the dispute between the West and the Soviet Union about Berlin is more than a narrow legal one concerned only with interpretations of texts and differences regarding the continuing validity of rights and duties. "The dispute cannot be understood," he said, "nor the prospects of using legal processes for its solution appraised, without taking account of the political background, for it is clear that the Berlin crisis involves wider purposes and policies of the protagonists, especially the Soviet Union."

To understand the significance of what the Russians are attempting to accomplish by precipitating a crisis in Berlin, Professor BOWIE continued, one must first understand what the Russians mean when they say they are following a policy of "peaceful coexistence." As Khrushchev and other Communist leaders interpret it, "peaceful coexistence" does not mean "live and let live"; it means continuing struggle to expand areas of Communist control by all means, political, economic, ideological, short of all-out war. In particular, the Soviet Union has not forsworn the use of force or of threats of force if these can be effective in achieving its purposes without undue risk of all-out war.

"In this context, Germany and Berlin present both problems and opportunities for the Soviets."

Professor BOWIE recalled that the Soviet Union's original hope of easy victory for Communism in Germany and western Europe had been dashed as a result of actions taken by the Western powers in Germany and in Europe itself. Western Europe has since revived from the chaos of war, and has joined the United States and Great Britain in the defensive NATO alliance; since 1950 the European countries themselves have been engaged in creating a western European community which includes the Federal Republic of Germany. In consequence, it has been a constant Soviet purpose for over a decade to weaken the NATO alliance and to disrupt cooperation among the western European countries themselves and with the United States.

Thus far, said Professor BOWIE, the Russians have failed in their purpose. The continued vitality of NATO and the emerging western European community have made hope of future Communist successes in Europe remote, and have begun to create for the Soviet Union the spectre of a strong Europe on its western borders. Continued Western presence in Berlin has added strain on the East German régime, already unpopular among the people of East Germany. Seen from the Soviet side, the growing unity of Europe is a serious obstacle to plans for Communist aggrandizement: It tends to reduce conflict among the "capitalist" powers in Europe, to reconcile political frictions and tensions among the European countries, and, with the United Kingdom a member of the community, to create a powerful new force in world politics.

At the same time, Professor BOWIE added, there has been in the Soviet Union a steady growth of economic and military power; indeed, the Soviet economy is growing at a rate almost twice that of the United States, especially in the field of heavy industry. The Russians have become persuaded that in military strength they are the defensive equal of the United States. It seemed to Professor BOWIE that these considerations have led the Soviets to believe that they might use this new strength, which they view as shifting the balance of forces, to weaken or undermine Western cohesion. To them, Berlin offers an occasion for the use of strength to this end. In particular it represents an opportunity for the Soviet Union to weaken the NATO alliance and to cast doubt throughout the world on the resolution of the West in the face of Soviet power. He recalled that, in essence, the Soviet proposals of 1958 were two: that the Western powers recognize East Germany as a legitimate state, which would make permanent the division of Germany; and that they agree to the severance of ties between West Berlin and the Federal Republic. These demands were made in the face of solemn and repeated declarations by the West to the Federal Republic and to West Berlin that the great powers would strive for the reunification of Germany on the basis of free elections, and that they would preserve West Berlin from absorption by the Communist bloc.

The Russians are attempting to use the issue of Berlin, Professor BOWIE continued, to convince the Federal Republic that the West can be coerced into recognizing the claims of the East German régime and the permanence of the division in Germany. It is enough for Soviet purposes if the Federal Republic is thus encouraged to seek greater independence in its foreign policy, for if it loses faith in the reliability of its Western partners, or in the adequacy of the NATO security system or the European community, there will have begun that erosion of bonds among the western European countries which the U.S.S.R. desires to see happen.

It is the further purpose of the Soviet Union, Professor BOWIE continued, to separate precariously positioned West Berlin from the Federal Republic and the Western world. Creation of a demilitarized free city would necessarily sever those ties which now exist between West Berlin and the Western countries, and upon which the city depends for physical security, economic well-being, and political freedom. Were the West to bow to Soviet threats of force, and allow West Berlin to be cut loose, the Russians would have succeeded in casting doubt on the resolve of the great powers to honor the commitments they have made to defend free peoples all over the world. Professor BOWIE continued:

"There is far more involved in the determination of the West to remain in Berlin than insistence upon observance of solidly

41

grounded legal rights. The reason we are prepared to stay in Berlin and to honor commitments which we have made to protect the people of Berlin is that, fundamentally, we must identify ourselves with the desire of other peoples to remain free.

"I think we have no moral right to give up our legal rights — even if we wanted to. Our presence in Berlin is by right, not by consent of the Soviets. But we are there also as partners of the people of West Berlin, to preserve their liberty jointly with them. If we don't understand this, we won't have the moral fiber to face what may be our ultimate responsibility — risking our own lives and fortunes for these two million people in Berlin.

"We must be prepared even for this, for we are not an island, nor are they an island; freedom is indivisible, and we must be prepared to fight for it wherever it is threatened. This is the ultimate reality: Our power is indissolubly linked with the freedom of these people, and we are the only ones able to vindicate the legal rights upon which that freedom depends."

Mr. McCLOY agreed that the West owed a profound duty to the people of West Berlin which goes beyond legal rights, saying:

"As I listened to this very lawyer-like discussion of the legal issues in the Berlin crisis, I couldn't help but think beyond the law to the human aspect of that city. It seems that there has always been a crisis in Berlin, and those of us who were there during some very trying times will always remember the spirit and courage of the people of West Berlin.

"Let me tell you about one time—in May, 1950, when the Blue Shirts, the Communist German Youth group, were being organized in the Soviet sector for what was intended to be a mass march on West Berlin to take over the city. We were so concerned about the intelligence of their intentions to use the occasion to take over the city that we reinforced our garrisons. I remember going up and talking to Burgomeister Reuter about it. He reminded me that when Charles V laid siege to Florence, the city had refused to surrender, and answered the cannon fire by ringing the bells of Florence to bring out the people to its defense. Reuter said: 'That is what I will do if these Blue Shirts should try to take our city.'

"On May Day Reuter did ring his bells, and he brought every-

42

body out. All the churches rang their bells, and all the municipal buildings — it was a signal for everybody in Berlin to turn out. In full view of the Blue Shirts marshalling on the other side, almost a million people moved up to the Tiergarten. I never saw a million people together until that day, but all of Berlin was there. It was much more than an effective gesture; it was really a physical impact. There was no Blue Shirt march on West Berlin after that demonstration."

Professor BOWIE, continuing his analysis of Soviet aims, observed that the Berlin crisis seemed to him yet another in a series of Soviet tactics designed to divide and weaken the West. He referred to recent Russian threats to Finland, and through her to the other Scandinavian countries; Communist attempts to revive in France and other European countries fear of the Germans by recollection of Nazi occupation brutality; the rousing in England of fears of German economic competition; and, finally, Soviet resumption of nuclear testing involving use of a fifty megaton weapon as a terror device.

If these are the considerations which move the Soviet Union, Professor BOWIE concluded, then the only final settlement of the Berlin question which it contemplates is one which would have the collateral effects outlined. Certainly the Soviet Union is not of a mind at this point to agree to those resolutions of the problem which the West would consider legitimate. "It seems to me, therefore, that the best we can hope for is some modus vivendi by which the West can, in an uneasy power balance, retain its basic position."

Mr. McCLOY agreed with Professor BOWIE that Berlin is unquestionably tied to ultimate Soviet objectives. He recalled discussing the Berlin situation with Khrushchev at a meeting on the Black Sea:

"I came away from that meeting feeling very strongly that if the Western governments — France, England, the Federal Republic, and the United States — had a clear, definite, united position with respect to Berlin, Khrushchev might well conform himself to it. His inclination to probe further in regard to alterations in the Berlin situation come, in my judgment, from his feeling that there is dissension and lack of unity about the subject among the Western governments."

43

It seemed to Dr. CONANT that for some time it has been the objective of the Soviet Union in talking about Berlin to attempt to give legal status to the puppet régime in East Germany, and thus to embarrass the Western powers, who have expressly declared that they consider the government of the Federal Republic the only government entitled to speak for Germany as the representative of the German people in international affairs.

Mr. SCHWARZ speculated that Khrushchev does not really intend to conclude a separate peace treaty with the East Germans, fearing to turn over real power to a puppet government without popular support, but that the Soviet leader uses the threat in an attempt to coerce Western compromise on Berlin.

4. The Role of Law in the Settlement of the Berlin Dispute

Mr. DEBEVOISE contended that no discussion of the role law can play in the settlement of the Berlin crisis should ignore the fact that the conflict involved the broad political interests of two powerful protagonists as well as legitimate legal questions. For its part the West has made it very clear that it is not interested merely in asserting legal rights in Berlin, but that it considers it has an obligation, and further that it is part of its vital interests, to protect the people of West Berlin in the freedom and way of life which that population has so strongly indicated its desire to retain. Russia, on its part, clearly hopes to use the Berlin question to weaken the Western alliance, among its members and in the eyes of the world. Hence it is impossible to discuss solely in terms of the legal issues a dispute between the two largest power blocs on earth.

Neither, in 1962, is it realistic to expect that the Berlin dispute will be settled by international adjudication. Although the International Court of Justice would have jurisdiction to render a judgment on the legal issues involved if the parties agreed to submit the case for such determination, it is hardly likely the U.S.S.R. will submit the Berlin question to the Court for final decision when it has refused to give the Court the authority to determine Soviet liability in the aerial incident cases. If the crisis were referred to the Security Council as a threat to world peace, the Council has power to ask for an advisory opinion from the Court on the legal questions at issue, but, Mr. DEBEVOISE pointed out, such a decision by the Security Council, if it be other than procedural, may be vetoed by one of the permanent members. In those circumstances the General Assembly might ask for an advisory opinion on the legal issues but in light of the difficult questions involved in the Berlin dispute the problem is not one which lends itself easily to complete solution by judicial process alone.

However, Mr. DEBEVOISE continued, the fact that the Berlin dispute is composed of political as well as legal issues does not diminish the importance of legal processes. It is noteworthy that even Mr. Khrushchev, whatever other ends he pursues in creating an international crisis over Berlin, has taken pains to justify the Soviet position on legal grounds. Mr. DEBEVOISE concluded:

> "The political aspects of the Berlin crisis ought not to diminish the importance of the legal issues involved, nor minimize the use of the role of law in its settlement. The world is trying to make progress towards the settlement of international disputes by means short of war; every member of the United Nations has undertaken to try to solve its international disputes by peaceful means. The West is presently exploring with the Soviet Union the possibilities of ending the Berlin crisis through negotiation — a use of the role of law rather than reliance upon naked force. As practicing lawyers know, it is important at the negotiating table to be able to argue from a strong, sound legal position. Furthermore, we persuade a watching world of the justice of our cause when we show that the rights which we assert are firmly based in law."

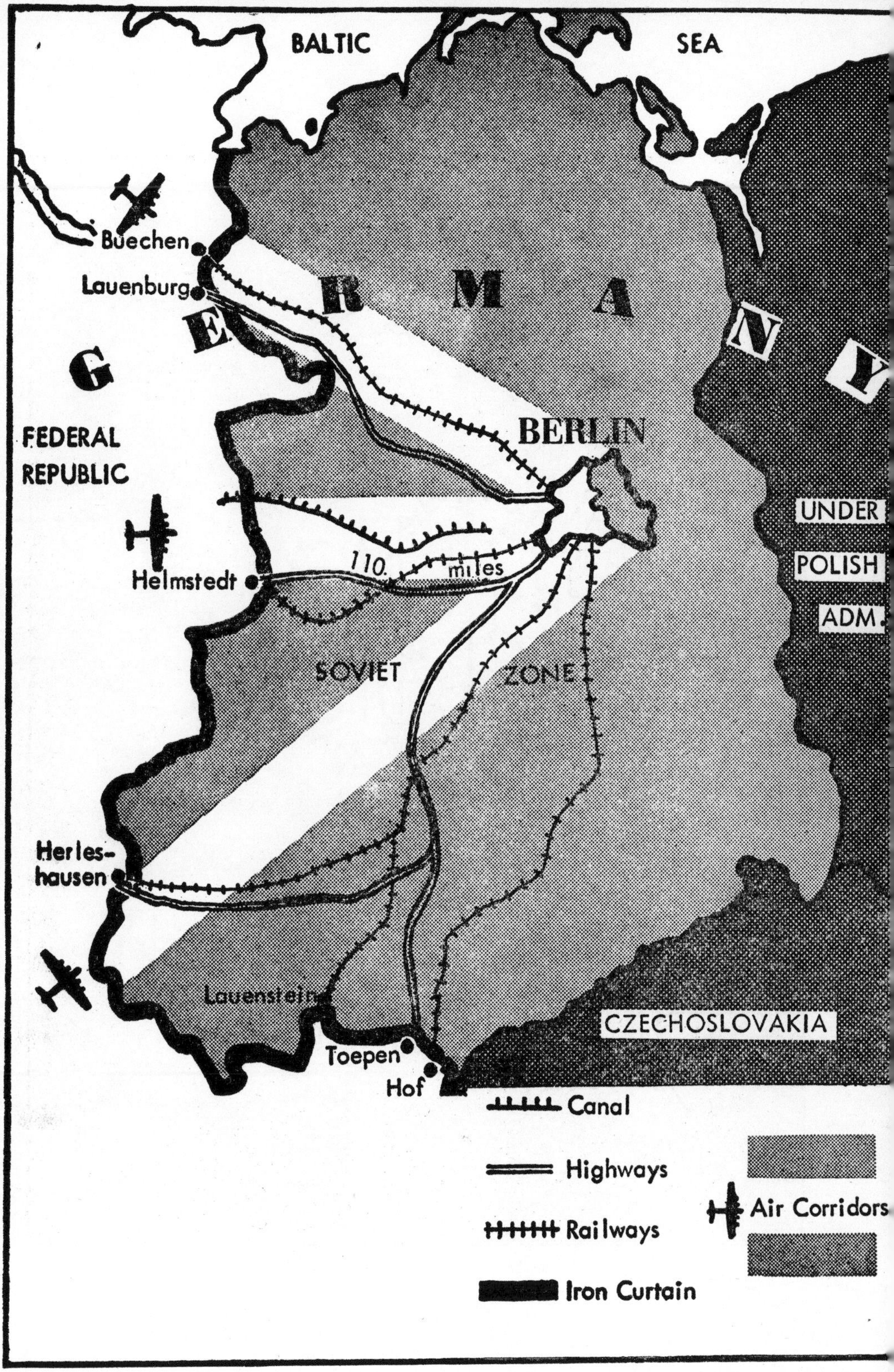
BALTIC
SEA
GERMANY
FEDERAL REPUBLIC
Buechen
Lauenburg
BERLIN
Helmstedt
110 miles
UNDER POLISH ADM.
SOVIET ZONE
Herleshausen
Lauenstein
Toepen
Hof
CZECHOSLOVAKIA
Canal
Highways
Railways
Iron Curtain
Air Corridors

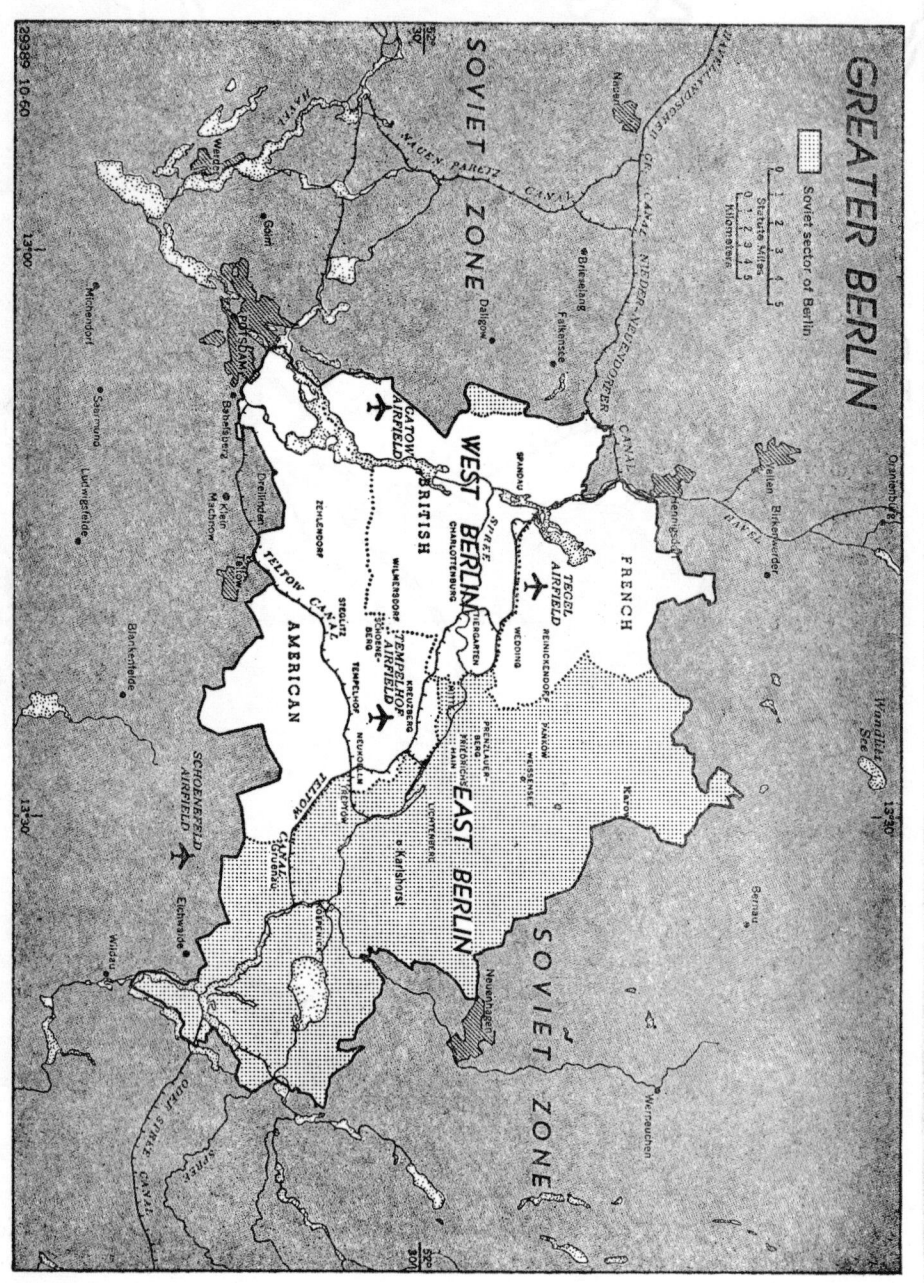

48

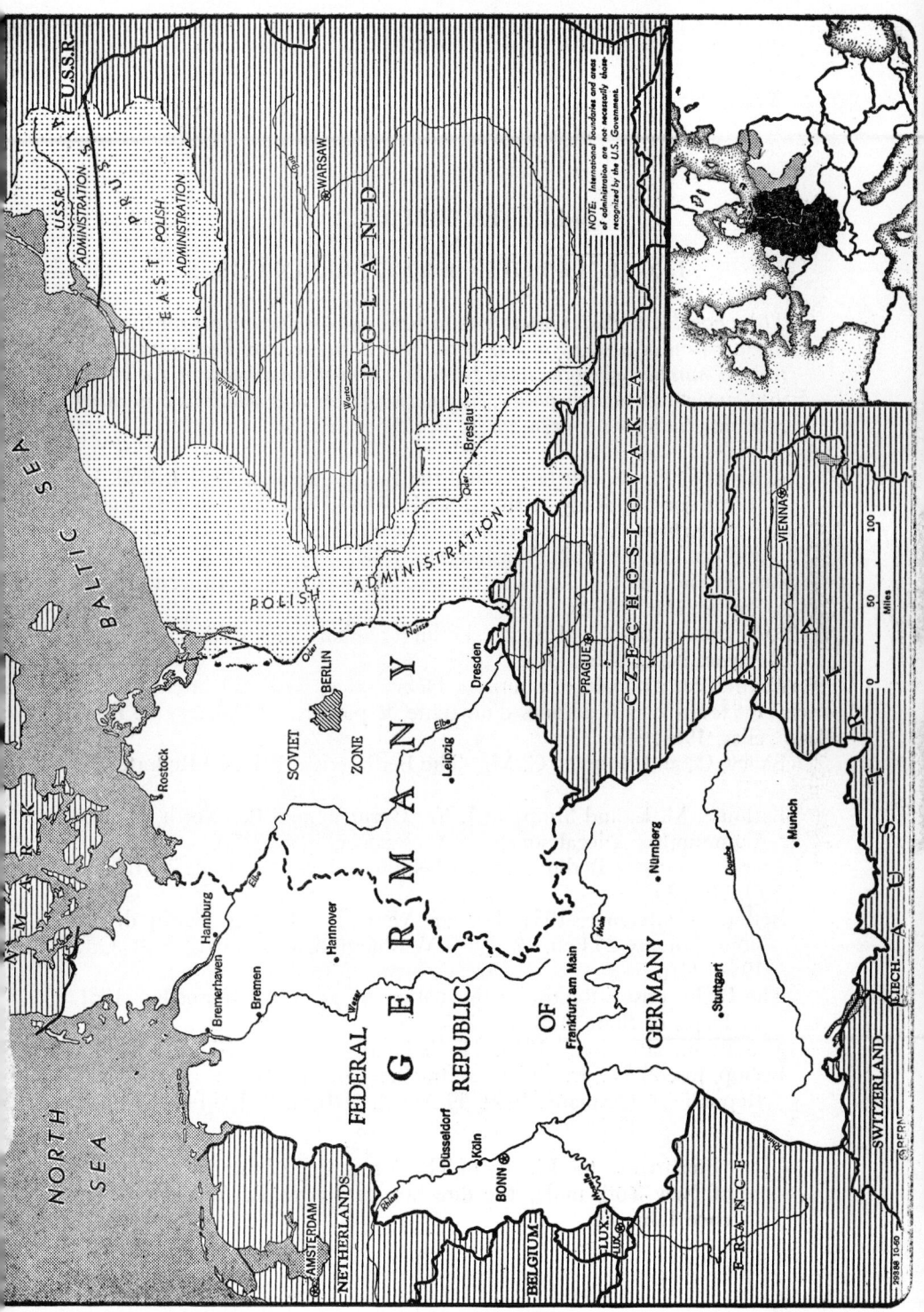

NOTE: International boundaries and areas of administration are not necessarily those recognized by the U.S. Government.

BALTIC SEA

NORTH SEA

U.S.S.R.

U.S.S.R. ADMINISTRATION

EAST PRUSSIA

POLISH ADMINISTRATION

WARSAW

P O L A N D

Breslau

Oder

Warta

POLISH ADMINISTRATION

Neisse

Oder

BERLIN

SOVIET ZONE

Dresden

Leipzig

Elbe

CZECHOSLOVAKIA

PRAGUE

VIENNA

Miles
0   50   100

Rostock

Hamburg

Elbe

Hannover

Bremerhaven

Bremen

Weser

F E D E R A L   G E R M A N Y   REPUBLIC   OF   GERMANY

Düsseldorf

Köln

BONN

Rhine

Frankfurt am Main

Main

Nürnberg

Danube

Stuttgart

Munich

A L P S

NETHERLANDS

AMSTERDAM

BELGIUM

LUX.

FRANCE

SWITZERLAND

CZECH.

BERN

49

SELECTED BIBLIOGRAPHY
ON THE
LEGAL ASPECTS OF THE BERLIN CRISIS*

This checklist includes references to basic offical documents on the Berlin question as well as recent periodical literature. As background material a number of works have been listed on some aspects of American diplomacy and foreign policy, international law and relations and other relevant studies on contemporary world politics.

Achminov, H.   Soviet tactics and the Berlin question. 1959. 6 Bull. Institute for the Study of the U.S.S.R. 34-41.

Am. Enterprise Assn.   Special analysis; the Berlin crisis. Pt. III, Legal and economic factors. Washington, 1961.

Am. Friends of the Captive Nations.   Questions and answers on the Berlin crisis. 1959.

Am. Universities Field Staff.   Berlin's symbols and realities, by E. A. Bayne. N.Y., 1960. 34p.

Assn. Internationale des Juristes Démocrates.   Recontre internationale sur les aspects juridiques d'un traite de paix avec L'Allemagne. Bruxelles, 1961. 51p.

Bailey, G. and Roberts, C. M.   The Berlin crisis, 1959. 20 Reporter 21-25.

Bathurst, M. E. and Simpson, J. F.   Germany and the North Atlantic Community: A legal survey. N.Y., Praeger, 1956. 217p.

Beerman, Hans.   Berlin: freedom behind barbed wire. 1961. 2 Midwest Q. 207-220.

Berlin.   Conference, 1954. Foreign Ministers Meeting—Berlin discussions, January 25-Feb. 18, 1954. Washington, U.S. Govt. Print. Off., 1954. 241p.

The Berlin crisis—Report to the nation by President Kennedy.   1961. 45 Dept. of State Bull. 267-273.

The Berlin situation.   1959. 11 External Aff. (Canada)2-6.

Bishop, Joseph W., Jr.   The "contractual agreements" with the Federal Republic of Germany. 1959. 49 Am. J. of Int'l. L. 125-147.

*Prepared by the Library of The Association of the Bar of the City of New York under the direction of Joseph L. Andrews, Reference Librarian.

Bishop, W.W. The international rule of law. 1961. 59 Mich. L. Rev. 553.

Bloomfield, L. P. Political gaming. Sept. 1960. U.S. Naval Inst. Proc. Towards a more lawful world—hopes and hazards. 1960. Am. Soc. Int'l. L. Proc. 71-77.

Bowett, D. W. Self-defense in international law. New York, Praeger, 1958.

Bowie, Robert R. Studies in federalism. Boston, Little, Brown, 1954.

Brandt, Willy. Von Bonn nach Berlin. Berlin, Arani, 1957. 175p. The East-West problem as seen from Berlin. 1958. 34 Int'l. Aff. 297-304.

The means short of war. 1961. 39 For. Aff. 196-207.

My road to Berlin. Garden City, N.Y., Doubleday, 1960. 287p.

Bridge, John F. Berlin:background for crisis. 1961. 158 Wall St. J. 10+

Clay, Lucius Du Bignon. Decision in Germany. 1st ed. Garden City, N.Y., Doubleday, 1950. 522p. Lecture on our stake in Europe and its effect on our role in Germany . . . at the House of the Association . . . . N.Y., 1949. 29p.

Cleveland, Harlan. ed. The promise of world tensions by Ralph J. Bunche, Adlai E. Stevenson, etc. N.Y., Macmillan, 1961. 157p.

Cogniot, G. La crise de Berlin. 1961. no. 99 Pensée (Paris) 3-25.

Cohen, Benjamin V. The United Nations: Constitutional developments, growth and possibilities. Cambridge, Harvard Univ. Press, 1961.

Conant, James B. Germany and freedom: a personal appraisal. Cambridge, Harvard Univ. Press, 1958. 117p. Our new partner—the Federal Republic of Germany. Washington, U.S. Dept. of State, 1955. 17p.

Conference of Foreign Ministers, Geneva, 1959. Principal documents. London, H.M. Stat. Off., 1959. 43p.

Conference on Ethical Values in International Decision Making. Institute of Social Studies, Hague, 1958. Hague, Martinus Nijhoff, 1960. 103p.

Corbett, Percy E. Morals, law and power in international relations, Los Angeles, The John Randolph Haynes and Dora Haynes Foundation, 1956. 51p.

Cordtz, Dan. West Berlin's plight: city loses workers, faces tourism decline, drop in retail sales. 1961. 158 Wall St. J. 1+.

Cornides. Berlin und was dann. 1961. 16 Europea Archiv 369-78.

Dahm, George. Volkerrecht Stuttgart, Kohlhammer, 1958-61, 2v.

Dallin, A. Soviet conduct in world affairs. N.Y. Columbia Univ. Press, 1960. 318p.

Davison, Walter Phillips. The Berlin blockade; a study in cold war politics. Princeton, N.J., Princeton Univ. Press, 1958. 423p.

Dehio, Ludwig. Germany and world politics in twentieth century. Trans. by Dieter Pevsner. New York, Alfred A. Knopf, 1959. 142p.

Dodd, T. J. German reunification—the present Berlin crisis. 1959. 25 Vital speeches of the day 328-332.

Donner, J. Report from Berlin. Trans. by A. T. Anderson, Bloomington, Indiana Univ. Press, 1961. 284p.

Dowling, W. C. Germany divided—the confrontation of two ways of life. 1961. 44 Dept. of State Bull. 588-591.

Drath, M. Berlin und Bonn. Die Rechtsiellung Berlin in der Bundesrepublik. 1951. 5 Juristische Rundschau 385.

Dulles, E. L. The challenge to the Western policy for Germany — the threat to Berlin. 1959. 25 Vital speeches of the day 324-328.

The meaning of Berlin for the free world. 1957. 36 Dept. of State Bull. 175-181.

The East and West must meet; a symposium. by Cora Du Bois and others. East Lansing, Michigan State Univ. Press, 1959. 134p.

East-West actions and reactions in Berlin. 19 Cong. Q. W. Rept. 1429. (Aug. 18, 1961)

East-West problems and negotiations, in Interparliamentary Union. 49th conference, Tokyo, 1960. Compte rendu. Genève, 1961. 322-337.

Eisenhower, Dwight D. West Berlin and the nation's defense. 1959. 25 Vital speeches of the day 354-357.

Eschenburg, Theodor. Die deutsche frage die Verfassungsprobleme der Wiedervereinigung. Munchen, R. Oldenbourg, 1959. 56p.

Faust, Fritz. Das Potsdamer Abkommen und seine völkerrechtliche Beduetung. Frankfurt am Main, A. Metzner, 1959. 201p.

Feis, Herbert. Between war and peace; the Potsdam Conference. N.J., Princeton Univ. Press, 1960. 367p.

Finletter, Thomas K. Foreign policy: the next phase. N.Y., Harper and Brothers, 1958. For the Council on Foreign Relations, 208p.

Fleming, D. F. The future of West Berlin. 1961. 14 Western Pol. Q. 37-48, pt.1.

What future for West Berlin? 1960. 9 For. Aff. Repts. (India) 33-44.

Foreign policy in world politics. 2d ed. R. C. Macridis, ed. Englewood Cliffs, N.J., Prentice-Hall, 1962. 480p.

France, U.K. and U.S. Protest travel restrictions in Berlin: issued by East German offlcials in violation of Four power agreements on Berlin. 1960. 43 Dept. of State Bull. 748-751.

Frei, Otto. The barrier across Berlin and its consequences. 1961. 17 World Today (London) 459-70.

Friedmann, Wolfgang G. Legal and political aspects of the Berlin crisis. 1961. Columbia Society of Int'l. L. Bull. 3-8.

Fulbright, J. William. American foreign policy in the 20th century under an 18th century constitution. 1961. 47 Cornell L. Q. 1-13.

Galay, N.Y. Berlin in the foreign policy of the CCCPSU. Analysis of current developments in the Soviet Union 1-8, May 5, 1959.

Gablentz, Otto Martin von der, ed. Documents on the status of Berlin 1944-1959. With a pref. by Willy Brandt. Munchen, R. Oldenbourg, 1959. 230p.

German Constitution—status of Berlin—reservation of Military Governors 1949—constitutionality of Berlin laws not reviewable by Federal Constitutional Court. 1958. 52 Am. J. of Int'l. L. 358-360.

German Embassy Press and Information Office. Situation in Berlin. May, 1959.

Geyelin, Philip. Kennedy and Berlin. 1961. 158 Wall St. J. 1+.

Gomulka, W. Poland's vital interest. 1961. 4 Polish Perspectives 3-8.

Goold, Adams R. Berlin and the situation in Europe. 1959. 2 J. Royal Commonwealth Soc. 65-68.

Gottlieb, Manuel. The German peace settlement and the Berlin crisis. N.Y., Paine-Whitman, 1960. 275p.

Great Britain. Papers by Command. Documents about the future of Germany (including Berlin)
Sept. to Dec. 1958. 1959. 27p. (Cmd. 634)
Jan. to Feb. 1959. (Germany No. 2 (1959) Cmd. 670)
March 2 to April 4, 1959. 1959. (Germany No. 3 (1959) Cmd. 719)

Green, L.C. Berlin and the U.N. 1949. 3 World Aff. 23-42.

Hazard, John N. Codifying peaceful co-existence. 1961. 55 Am. J. Int'l, L. Legal research on peaceful co-existence. 1957. 51 Am. J. Int'l. L.

Henkin, Louis. The Berlin crisis and the United Nations. N.Y., Carnegie Endowment for Int'l. Peace. 1959. 30p.

Holbrook, Sabra. Capital without a country; the challenge of Berlin. Coward-McCann, 1961 . 121p.

Hottelet, R. C. Berlin and beyond. 1961. 5 Orbis (Philadelphia) 267-91.

Hudson, G. F. Berlin—the menaced city. 1959. 27 Commentary 311-316.

Institute for International Order. Current thought on peace and war ...N.Y., 1960 to date.

Jessup, Philip C. Review of Allied action in Berlin Blockade. 1948. 19 Dept. of State Bull. 541-547.
The rights of the United States in Berlin. 1949. 43 Am. J. Int'l. L. 92-95.
The use of international law. Ann Arbor, Univ. of Michigan Law School, 1959. 164p. (The Thomas M. Cooley Lectures, 8th series)

Kaplan, Morton. System and process in international politics. N.Y., Wiley, 1957. 283p.

Kaplan, Morton A. and Katzenbach, Nicholas DeB. The patterns of international politics and of international law. 53 Am. Pol. Science Rev. 693-712.

The political foundations of international law. N.Y., Wiley, 1961. 372p.

Katz, Milton. International disputes: an address. 1960. 54 of the Am. Soc. of Int 'l. L. proc. 254-261.

Kelsen, Hans. The legal status of Germany according to the Declaration of Berlin. 1945. 39 Am. J. of Int'l. L. 518-526.

Kennan, George F. Russia; the atom and the west. N.Y., Harper, 1958. 116p.

Kerstein, J. Die Deutsche Demokratische Republik ein Staat im Sinne des Volkerrechts. 1957. 6 Staat und Recht 249-260.

Kertesz, Stephen D. and Fitzsimons, M.A. Diplomacy in a changing world. Notre Dame, Indiana Univ. Press, 1959. 407p.

Khrushchev's press conference on German problem. 1959. 11 Current digest of the Soviet press 12-16.

King, J. E. The Berlin controversy—What are we prepared to defend? 1959. 140 New Republic 10-15.

Kissinger, Henry A. Nuclear weapons and foreign policy. Foreword by Gordon Dean. N.Y., Harper & Brothers for Council on For. Rel., 1957. 455p.

Kircheimer, Otto. The administration of justice and the concept of legality in East Germany. 1959. 68 Yale L. J. 705-749.

Klimow, Gregory. The terror machine; the inside story of the Soviet administration in Germany. Trans. from the German by H. C. Stevens. Introduced by Edward Crankshaw and Ernst Reuter. N.Y. Praeger, 1953. 400p.

Kröger, H. Das Potsdamer. Abkommen: eine internationale Rechtsgrundlage des deutschen Volkes. 1960. 9 Staat und Recht 1456-1482.

Die rechtlichen Grundlagen der sowjetischen Vorschläge zur Lösung der Berliner Frage. 1959. 4 Deutsche Aubenpolitik 14.

Zu den Rechtsguendlagen der sowjetischenVorschläge für die Lösung der Berliner Frage. 1959. 8 Staat und Recht 1.

Zu einigen Fragen des staatsrechtlichen Status von Berlin. 1958. 3 Deutsche Aubenpolitik 10.

Kuhn, Ferdinand. The facts behind the Berlin crisis. (Reprint from Washington Post, Oct. 4-5, 1948)

Larson, Arthur. Peace through law: the role and limits of adjudication—some contemporary applications. World Rule of Law Center, Duke Univ. School of Law. 1960. 8p. (World Rule of Law Booklet Series, no. 5)

When nations disagree: a handbook on peace through law. Louisiana State University Press, 1961. 251p.

Lebedev, V. P. Berlin through Soviet eyes. 1961. 2 Atlas (New York) 271-73.

Legal aspects of the Berlin situation. 1959. 40 Dept. of State Bull. 5-13.

Legaret, J. Berlin. 1961. 50 Revue politique des idées et des institutions 345-351.

Legien, R. Les Accords quadripartites sur Berlin. Berlin, 1960. 63p.
The four power agreements on Berlin: Alternative solutions to the Status Quo? Trans. by Trevor Davies. Foreword by Franz Amrehn. Berlin, Carl Heymanns Verlag, 1960. 69p.

Leprette, J. Le Status de Berlin. 1955. 1 Annuaire Français de Droit International 123-127.

Lie, Trygve. In the cause of peace. N.Y., Macmillan, 1954. Chapter XII. Mediation in Berlin pp. 199-218.

Lipsky, George A., ed. & comp. Law and politics in the world community. Essays on Hans Kelsen's Pure Theory and Related Problems in International Law. Berkeley & Los Angeles. Univ. of California. 1953. 373p.

Litchfield, Edward Harold. Governing postwar Germany. Ithaca, Cornell Univ. Press, 1953. 661p.

Loventin, A. V. The myth of international security. Jerusalem, Mayner Press, 1960. 346p.

Lowenstein, Karl. The Allied presence in Berlin: legal basis. 1959. 38 For. Policy Bull.

McClellan, Grant S. The two Germanies. N.Y., H. W. Wilson, 1959. 184p.

McClure, Wallace. World legal order: possible contributions by the people of the United States. Chapel Hill, Univ. of North Carolina Press. 366p.

McDougal, Myres S. and Florentino P. Feliciano. Law and minimum world public order: the legal regulation of international coercion. New Haven, Yale Univ. Press, 1961.
Studies in world public order. New Haven, Yale Univ. Press, 1961.

McInnis, Edgar and others. The shaping of postwar Germany. London, J. M. Dent for Canadian Institute of International Affairs, 1960. 195p.

Meier, V. At the crossroad of two worlds. Aug. 1961. Swiss Rev. of Int'l. Aff.

Morgenthau, Hans J. The problem of German reunification. 1960. 330 Am. Academy of Pol. and Social Science, The Annals. 124-132.

Mosely, Philip Edward. The Kremlin and world politics: studies in

Soviet policy and action. N.Y., Vintage Books, 1960. 557p.

Munch, Fritz. Berlin. (In Strupp, Karl, Worterbuch des Volkerrechts ...Berlin, 1960, Vol. I, pp. 182-184)

Munro, Leslie. The Berlin crisis and the need for a U.N. Police Force. Am. Bar Assn. Section of Int'l. and Comparative Law. Proceedings, Bal Harbour, Miami Beach, Florida. August 24, 25, 1960. 22-27.

Neal, Fred Warner. War and peace and the problem of Berlin. Claremont Grad. School California.

Netti, J. P. The Eastern Zone and Soviet policy in Germany, 1945-50. London, Oxford Univ. Press, 1951. 324p.

Nollaw, G. International communism and world revolution history and methods. N.Y. Praeger, 1961. 357p.

Organski, A. F. K. Berlin and two Germanies. 1959. 36 Current History 200-204.

Les Origines du problème de l'accés à Berlin—Quest. 662 Perspectives 5.

Padelford, Norman J. Report on political exercise on Berlin crisis. 1959 (Cambridge) Pol. Sec. M.I.T. 22.

Patterson, William D. Berlin: the cradle and the lever. 1961. Nov. 25 Saturday Rev. 19.

Pinto, Roger. The international status of the German Democratic Republic (reprinted from an article with the same title in the Journal du Droit International of Paris, No. 2/1959 on behalf of Deutsche Aussenpolitik). 104p.

Plischke, Elmer. Berlin: development of its government and administration. Historical Division, Office of the Executive Secretary, Office of U.S. High Commissioner for Germany, 1952. 257p.

E possibile un compromesso su Berlino? 1961. 28 Riv. di Studi Politici Internazionali (Firenze) 323-28.

Princeton University. Center of International Studies. World Politics. Special Issue, Oct. 1961.

Prittie, Terence. Germany divided. Boston, Little, Brown, 1960. 381p.

Report by Chairman N. S. Khrushchev on his meeting with President John F. Kennedy in Vienna. N.Y., Cross Current Press, 1961.

Resolving the Russian-American deadlock, ed. by James C. Charlesworth in 324 Annals of Am. Acad. July 1959.

Robson, Ed. Berlin: pivot of German destiny. Chapel Hill, Univ. of North Carolina Press, 1960. 233p.

Rothfels, Hans. Berlin in vergangenheit und gegenwart; Tubinger Vortrage. Tubingen, Mohr, 1961. 158p.

Ruhm, von Oppen Beate. Documents on Germany under occupation, 1945-1954. London, Oxford Univ. Press, 1955. 660p.

Schwarzenberger, Georg. The impact of East-West rift in international law. 1950. 36 Grotius Soc. Transactions 229-269.

A manual of international law. 4th ed. N.Y. Praeger, 1960. 2v.

Schwoebel, Jean. La question de Berlin. Esprit, mars 1960. pp. 468-472.

Silvain, R. Berlin, une négociation très discrète. 1959. 226 Revue politique et parlementaire 312-320.

Simpson, J. L. Berlin: Allied rights and responsibilities in the divided city. 1957. 6 Int'l. & Comp. L. Q. 83-102.

Smith, Bruce L. R. The governance of Berlin. 1959. 525 Int'l. Conciliation (entire issue)

Snell, John L. Dilemma over Germany. New Orleans, Hauser Press, 1961.

The Soviet bloc and West Germany. 1961. 10 East Europe 3-10.

Soviet efforts for the solution of the questions of Berlin and West Berlin, Nov. 1958. 1959. London, Soviet Booklet 46, 53.

The Soviet Stand on Germany. Crosscurrents Press, Inc., 1961.

Speier, Hans. Divided Berlin: the anatomy of Soviet political blackmail. N. Y., Praeger, 1961. 201p.

The Soviet threat to Berlin. Santa Monica, Calif., Rand Corp., 1960. 67p.

Les statut international de Berlin. 1 Chron. Pol. et Etr. 75-95.

Stein, E. Ist die Deutsche Demokratische Republik ein Staat. 85 Archiv des offentlichen Rechts 363-391, Heft. 4, 1960.

Stevenson, Adlai E. Putting first things first. N.Y., Random House. 1960.

Stolper, Wolfgang F. Germany between East and West. Washington, Nat'l. Plan. Assn., 1960. 80p.

Stone, Julius. Quest for survival; the role of law and policy. Cambridge, Harvard Univ. Press, 1961.

Strang, Lord. Germany between East and West. 1955. 33 For. Aff. 387-401.

Strauss, Franz-Josef. Soviet aims and German unity. 1959. 37 For. Aff. 366-377.

Tounkine. La traité de paix allemand et le droit international. 1961. No. 163 Etudes Sovetiques 26-29.

Tunkin, Gregory I. Co-existence and international law. 95 Hague Academy, Recueil des Cours (1958 III)

The Berlin problem and international law. 1959. Int'l. Aff. (Moscow) 36-43.

The two Europes (in Interparliamentary Union, 49th conference, Tokyo, 1960. Compte rendu. Genève, 1961. 338-353)

U.S. Dept. of State. American foreign policy. basic documents, 1950-1955. Washington, U.S. Govt. Print. Off., 1957. 2v.

Background of Heads of Government Conference, 1960: principal documents, 1955-1959. Washington, 1960. 478p.

The Soviet note on Berlin: an analysis. Washington, 1959. 53p.

Summaries of the contractual agreements with Germany and supporting documents. Texts of a Protocol to the North Atlantic treaty and
the Tripartite declaration issued at the signing of the European defense community treaty at Paris. Washington, U.S. Govt. Print. Off.,
1952. 32p.

U.S. Dept. of State. Division of Research for Western Europe. Chronology of events bearing on West German foreign affairs. May 5, 1955
to April 30, 1956. Wash., 1956. 20p.

U.S. Dept. of State. Historical Division. The Conference of Berlin;
the Potsdam Conference, 1945. Washington, U.S. Govt. Print. Off.,
1960. 2v.

Documents on Germany, 1944-1959. Background documents on
Germany, 1944-1959 and a chronology of political developments affecting Berlin 1945-1956. Wash., U.S. Govt. Print. Off., 1959. 491p.

Foreign Ministers Meeting. May-August 1959, Geneva documentary
publication. Wash., 1959. 603p.

U.S. Dept. of State. Office of Public Services. Berlin: city between two
worlds; background. Rev. Washington, 1960. 22p.

The Berlin crisis: report to the nation by President Kennedy. July
25, 1961.

Berlin—1961; background. Washington, 1961. 48p.

U.S. Treaties, etc. 1953- . Germany, boundary between United States
sector of Berlin and Soviet zone of occupation. Agreement between
the United States of America and the Union of Soviet Socialist Republics, signed at Berlin June 25, 1955. Wash., U.S. Govt. Print. Off.,
1956. 2p.

United States of America—United Kingdom—Union of Soviet Socialist Republics. Protocol on the zones of occupation in Germany and
the administration of "Greater Berlin" signed at London, Sept. 12,
1944, in force Feb. 6, 1945. 1960. 54 Am. J. Int'l. L. 739-741.

United States urges Soviet Union to conclude settlement of problems
of Germany and Berlin on basis of self-determination: statement made
by President Kennedy on July 19 on the subject of Germany and
Berlin . . . 1961. 45 Dept. of State Bull. 223-33.

Vicker, Ray. Approach to Berlin: Western Allies rely on economic
moves as well as arms buildup. 1961. 158 Wall St. J. 1+.

Warburg, James Paul. Germany: key to peace. Cambridge, Harvard
Univ. Press, 1953. 344p.

Wehberg. Theory and practice of international policing.

Wengler, W. International law problems of the situation of Germany.
1959. 15 Revue Egyptienne de Droit International 1.

58

Winter, Bernard. Berlin enjou et symbole. Paris, Calman-Levy, 1959. 190p.

Wiskemann, E. Berlin between East and West. 1960. 16 World Today 463-472.

World justice through law: a symposium. 1961. 56 Northwestern Univ. 1-175.

Ydit, Méir. Internationalised territories: from the free city of Cracow to the free city of Berlin. Leyden, A. W. Sythoff, 1961. 323 p.

Zink, Harold. The United States in Germany, 1944-1945. Princeton, Van Nostrand, 1957. 374p.

Zur frage eines frieden vertrages mit beiden deutschen Staaten äussern sich. 1961. 6 Deutscher Aussenpolitik (Berlin) 1165-1176.

Supplement to the Bibliography

January 15, 1963

Adenauer, Konrad. The German problem, a world problem. 1962. 41 For. Aff. 59-65

Alekseeve, Pyotr.
Delay is dangerous; the Soviet view on the German problem. Questions answered. London, Soviet Booklets. 1962. 23p.
Une question urgente, la conclusion du traité de paix allemand. Jan. 1962. Etudes Soviétiques 1-31 (no. 166-1st suppl.).

Answer to the Soviet memorandum of December 27, 1961: unabridged text of the answer of the German federal government. 1962. 7 (1) Germany i-vi.

Berlin. Nov. 27, 1961. Documentation francaise, Notes et études documentaires (no. 2836) 1-32.

Berlin and the German question. Munich, Arbeitskreis fur Ostfragen. 1962. 31p.

Berlin, summer 1961: five on the spot reports. Summer 1961. 2 Atlas 179-89.

Berlin (West Berlin). Federal Republic of Germany. Senator of the interior. Memorandum: eastern underground activity against west Berlin. April 15, 1959. 71 † 19p.; first suppl., 1960, 48p.

Bouscaren, A.T. Soviet foreign policy; a pattern of persistence. New York, Fordham Univ. Press. 1962. 187p.

Bretscher, W. Lessons of the Berlin crisis. Feb. 1962. 11 Swiss Rev. of World Aff. 1-3.

Bundy, McGeorge. Policy for the western alliance—Berlin and after. 1962. 46 Dep't State Bull. 419-25.

Clay, Lucius D. Berlin. 1962. 41 For. Aff. 47-58.

La crise allemande—le point de vue de la Pologne. Oct. 1961. 4 Perspectives Polonaises 3-10.

The crisis over Berlin June-August 1961 (in Documents on American foreign relations 1961. N.Y., Harper & Bros. for Council on foreign relations. 1962. pp. 137-61)

The debate over Berlin (in Stebbins, Richard P., The United States in world affairs 1960. N.Y., Harper & Bros. for Council on foreign relations. 1961. pp. 78-83)

De Kwestie—Berlijn in dokumenten. 1961. 15 Internationale Spectator 547-95.

60

Dix-sept ans de crise—une résumé chronologique des événements de Berlin depuis la deuxième guerre mondiale jusqu'au 21 septembre 1961. Oct. 1961. 10 Monde Combattant 15-18.

Erler, F.   Les aspects politiques de l'action soviétiques à Berlin. 1962. 27 (1) Politique Etrangère 5-14.

Flight rules by allied control authority.   Air directorate concerning air corridors in Germany and Berlin control zone, Oct. 22, 1946 (in U.S. dep't of state, Historical office, Documents on Germany 1944-51. Wash. 1961. pp. 63-72)

German Democratic Republic. Ministry of Foreign Affairs. The problem of West Berlin and solutions proposed by the government of the German democratic republic; with relevant documents. 3d enl. ed. Aug. 1961. 108p.

German Information Center.   Berlin: crisis and challenge. 1962. 67p.

Germany and Berlin before the summit (in Docements on American foreign relations 1960. N.Y., Harper & Bros. for Council on foreign relations. 1961. pp.106-13)

Germany and Berlin after the summit conference (in Documents on American foreign relations 1960. N.Y., Harper & Bros. for Council on foreign relations. 1961. pp.176-82)

Germany and the Berlin crisis (in Documents on international affairs 1958. 1962. pp. 137-72)

Graefrath, Bernhard.   Berlin air access sovereignty claimed by East Germany. Jan. 23, 1962. 4 + 15p. (SS-E) (Joint Publications Research Sev. series 12064)

Great Britain.   Documents about the future of Germany (including Berlin). June to July 1961. (Cmnd 1451)

Great Britain. Secretary of State for Foreign Affairs. Selected documents on Germany and the question of Berlin 1944-61. London, HMSO. 1961. 483p. (Cmnd 1552)

Grewe, Wilhelm G.   Germany and Berlin; an analysis of the 1959 Geneva conference with documents. Washington, Press & Information Off., German Embassy. 1960. 38p.

Healey, Denis.   The crisis in Europe. April 1962. 38 Int'l Aff. 145-55.

Herder, G.   Berlin was no fifth zone of occupation (in German). 1962. 11 Staat und Recht 47-51.

Herder, G. and Schneider, W.   Stationing armed forces of imperialist western powers in west Germany and west Berlin and riding airlines to west Berlin by the western powers are contrary to international law (in German). 1961. 10 Staat und Recht 2067-77.

International Commission of Jurists. The Berlin wall: a defiance of human rights. 1962. 54p.

International Institute for Peace. Dep't of Reference and Research. On the conclusion of a German peace treaty and settlement of the west Berlin problem. Vienna. 1961. 60p. (Current docs. and papers on international problems relative to world peace, no. 42).

Interview with Secretary of State Rusk, Aug. 29, 1961; extract (in U.S. dep't of state. Historical office. Documents on Germany 1944-61. Wash. 1961. pp. 744-50)

Interview with Secretary of State Rusk, concerning the situation in Berlin, July 23, 1961; extracts (in U.S. dep't of state Historical office. Documents on Germany 1944-61. Wash. 1961. pp.689-93)

Javits, Jacob K. A proposal for taking the initiative in Berlin. Dec. 21, 1961. 25 Reporter 21-3.

Khrushchev, Nikita S. Soviet policy on Germany; "we propose peace ..." Speeches of N.S. Khrushchev and documents of the Soviet government, June to Sept. 1961. London, Soviet Booklets. 1961. 91p.

Komarov, M. Co-existence of the two German states and the peace treaty. July 1962. Int'l Aff. (Moscow) 6-10.

The legal aspects of the Berlin situation: memorandum issued by the department of state Dec. 19, 1958 (in U.S. dep't of state. Historical off. American foreign policy 1958. Wash. 1962. pp.603-15)

Mackintosh, J.M. Strategy and tactics of Soviet foreign policy. London, Oxford Univ. Press. 1962. 332p.

Madre, J. de. West of the wall. 1961. 9 (10) NATO Letter 5-9.

Mander, John. Berlin, hostage for the west. Baltimore, Penguin Books. 1962. 124p.

Mansfield, M.J. A third way on Berlin. 1961. 5 NATO's Fifteen Nations 49-55.

Mezerik, Avrahm G., ed. Berlin and Germany: Berlin crisis, wall, free city, separate treaty, cold chronology. New York, International Review Serv. 1962. 93p.

Miksche, F.O. To die for Berlin? Blockade is the answer. 1962. 6 (7) NATO's Fifteen Nations 20-5.

Mosely, Philip E. The occupation of Germany: new light on how the zones were drawn. 1950. 28 For. Aff. 580-604.

Munch, Fritz. The German problem. 1962. 89 J. Droit Int'l 7-51.

Neal, F.W. War and peace and Germany. New York, W.W. Norton. 1962. 166p.

Polyanov, N. Soviet report on west Berlin, illusion and reality. March 14, 1962. (SS-E) (Joint Publications Research Serv. series 12942)

Pounds, N.J.G. Divided Germany and Berlin. Princeton, N.J., D. Van Nostrand. 1962. 128p.

Reintanz, G. Der kalte krieg, Westberlin und das volkerrecht. Jan. 1962. 11 Staat und Recht 26-47.

Report to the nation on the Berlin crisis by president Kennedy July 25, 1961 (in U.S. dep't of state. Historical off. Documents on Germany 1944-61. Wash. 1961, pp.694-700)

Riesman, David. Dealing with the Russians over Berlin. Winter 1961/ 62. 31 Am. Scholar 13-39.

Rose, Jonathan William. The Berlin crisis of 1958; the calculated risk of the Soviet Union. Chicago, Czechoslovak Foreign Institute in Exile. 1960. 53p.

Rostow, Walt Whitman. The present stage of the cold war. 1962. 47 Dep't State Bull. 675-82.

Rusk, Dean. Berlin et les états-unis. 1961. 16 (cahier 79) Etudes Américaines 1-12.

Schulz, Klaus-Peter. Berlin zwischen freiheit und diktatur. Berlin, Staneck. 1962. 576p.

The siege of west Berlin: fifteen years of divided Germany. March 1961. Round Table 160-5.

Skowronski, A.
Legal problems of the occupation status of greater Berlin. 1961. 8 Rev. Contemp. Law. 73-87.
The peace treaty with Germany and the problem of the so-called access of the three powers to west Berlin (in Polish). 1961. 14 (9) Sprawy Miedzynarodowe 12-34.
Problémes juridiques relatifs au statut d'occupation du grand-Berlin. June 1961. 8 Rev. Droit Contemporain 75-89.

Slezák, K. The status of west Berlin (in Czech). 1962. 101 Pravnik 17-29.

The Soviet Union and the right of peoples and nations to self-determination; a contribution to the German question. Bonn, Federal Ministry for All-German Questions. 1962. 28p.

Struye, P. La crise de Berlin. Jan/Feb. 1962. 61 Rev. Société d'Etudes & d'Expansion 111-26.

Tolplitz, H. Time for a German peace treaty. 1962. 1 Law & Legis. in German Democratic Republic 5-31.

U.S. Congress. House. Comm. on Foreign Affairs. (87.2) Sense of Congress with respect to Berlin. Report . . . to accompany H. Con. Res. 570, Oct. 3, 1962. Washington, Gov't Print. Off. 1962. 3p.

U.S. Congress. Senate. Comm. on Foreign Relations. (87.2) Expressing sense of Congress with respect to situation in Berlin. Report . . . to accompany S. Con. Res. 97, Oct. 10, 1962. Washington, Gov't Print. Off. 1962. 2p.

U.S. Department of State. Historical Office. Documents on Germany 1944-61. Comm. on foreign relations, U.S. senate. Washington, Gov't Print. Off. 1961. 833p.

U.S. note documents western position on unrestricted air access to Berlin: text of a U.S. note to the Soviet Union which was delivered by the American embassy at Moscow on Sept. 8, 1961. 1961. 45 Dep't State Bull. 511-15.

Villey, Daniel. La question de Berlin. Paris, Editions de l'Epargne. 1961. 38p.

Wagner, W. The development of the Berlin problem. 1961. 6 (5) NATO's Fifteen Nations 16-21.

Wall, R.F. The German question and the position of Berlin (in Barraclough, G., Survey of international affairs 1956-58. London, New York, Oxford univ. press. for royal inst. of international affairs. 1962. pp.574-88)

War of nerves over Berlin (in Stebbins, Richard P., The United States in world affairs 1961. N.Y., Harper & Bros. for Council on foreign relations. 1962. pp. 77-88)

Wehmeyer, D.A. Certain aspects of the German problem. Dec. 11, 1961. 45 Dep't State Bull. 968-73.

Windsor, P. Berlin crisis. 1962. 12 History Today 375-84.

Worsthorne, Peregrine. The Berlin crisis through British eyes. Nov. 23, 1961. 25 Reporter 35-6.

Wright, Quincy. Some legal aspects of the Berlin crisis. 1961. 55 Am. J. Int'l L. 959-65.

Zourek, J. The problem of western Berlin in the light of international law (in Czech). 1962. 6 Casopis pro Mezinárodní Právo 1-19.

NOTES
to
The Legal Background
of the Berlin-German Crisis

[1]See German Act of Military Surrender, May 8, 1945, in Senate Comm. on Foreign Relations, A *Decade of American Foreign Policy: Basic Documents, 1941-1949*, S. Doc. No. 123, 81st Cong., 1st Sess. 505 (1950) [hereinafter cited as A Decade of American Foreign Policy], U.S. Dep't of State and Staff of Senate Comm. on Foreign Relations, 86th Cong., 1st Sess., Documents on Germany, 1944-1959, 12 (Comm. Print 1959) [hereinafter cited as Documents on Germany, 1944-1959]; Declaration Regarding the Defeat of Germany and the Assumption of Supreme Authority by the Allied Powers, June 5, 1945. A Decade of American Foreign Policy 506, Documents on Germany, 1944-1959, 13. Soviet Foreign Minister Gromyko said on June 2, 1959, at the Geneva Foreign Ministers Meeting: "We do not think that the American, British and French troops were in Berlin in any sense unlawfully." U.S. Dep't of State, Foreign Ministers Meeting, May-August 1959, Geneva, 239 (1959) [hereinafter cited as 1959 Geneva Foreign Ministers Meeting].

[2]The formula of unconditional surrender was determined upon at least as early as 1943 by all three powers. See Declaration by the Governments of the United States, the United Kingdom, the Soviet Union, and China, on General Security, Nov. 1, 1943, A Decade of American Foreign Policy 11.

[3]See Mosely, *The Occupation of Germany*, 28 Foreign Affairs 580, 587 (1950), who adds: "A further factor favorable to making Berlin the seat of Allied authority was that any proposal to create a new capital, especially one situated in a western zone, seemed bound to meet with unrelenting Soviet opposition."

[4]At the Moscow Conference of Foreign Ministers in October, 1943, it was decided in anticipation of Germany's defeat to establish a European Advisory Commission of representatives appointed by the Heads of the Governments of the United States, the United Kingdom, and the U.S.S.R., the purpose of which was to recommend to the three governments terms of surrender for Germany and the means of enforcing Allied policy in conquered Germany based on an assumption of joint responsibility for policy and joint occupation. See Anglo-Soviet American Communiqué, Nov. 1, 1943, A Decade of American Foreign Policy 9, 10; Mosely, *supra* note 3, at 580-83. The three major Allied agreements

prepared by the European Advisory Commission were the September 12, 1944 Protocol on Zones of Occupation and the Administration of Greater Berlin, the November 14, 1944 Agreement on Control Machinery in Germany, and the June 5, 1945 Declaration Regarding the Defeat of Germany, with their amendments.

[5]Protocol between the United States, the United Kingdom, and the U.S.S.R. on the zones of occupation in Germany and the administration of "Greater Berlin," signed at London, Sept. 12, 1944, 5 U.S.T. 2078 T.I.A.S. No. 3071, 227 U.N.T.S. 279, in Documents on Germany, 1944-1959, at 1. The Protocol was amended on November 14, 1944 to modify the descriptions of the northwestern and southwestern zones and to specify their allocation to the United Kingdom and the United States respectively; no change was made in those provisions of the Protocol which related to the eastern zone allotted to the U.S.S.R. or to the administration and joint occupation of Berlin. Agreement between the United States, the United Kingdom, and the U.S.S.R. regarding amendments to the Protocol of 12 September 1944, signed at London, Nov. 14, 1944, 5 U.S.T. 2078, T.I.A.S. No. 3071, 227 U.N.T.S. 286, in Documents on Germany, 1944-1959, at 3. The Protocol as amended was approved by the United Kingdom on December 5, 1944, by the United States on February 2, 1945, and by the Soviet Union on February 6, 1945, whereupon it entered into force. The Protocol on Zones of Occupation was again amended on July 26, 1945, to include France among the occupying powers and carve out a French zone of occupation in Germany and a French sector of occupation in Berlin from the American and British zones and sectors, but the amendments effected no change as between the U.S.S.R. and the Western powers in the fundamental allocation of authority in Germany. Agreement between the United States, the U.S.S.R., the United Kingdom, and France regarding amendments to the Protocol of 12 September 1944 on the zones of occupation in Germany and the administration of "Greater Berlin," signed at London, July 26, 1954, 5 U.S.T. 2078, T.I.A.S. No. 3071, 227 U.N.T.S. 297, in Documents on Germany, 1944-1959, at 21.

[6]Protocol, *supra* note 5, para. 1.

[7]Agreement between the United States, the United Kingdom, and the U.S.S.R. on control machinery in Germany, signed at London, Nov. 14, 1944, 5 U.S.T. 2062, T.I.A.S. No. 3070, 236 U.N.T.S. 359, in Documents on Germany, 1944-1959, at 5. The agreement was approved by the United Kingdom on December 5, 1944, by the United States on January 24, 1945, and by the Soviet Union on February 6, 1945, whereupon it entered into force. The instrument was amended on May 1, 1945 to provide for the participation of France in the Allied control machinery. Amending Agreement between the United States, the United

66

Kingdom, the U.S.S.R., and the Provisional Government of France, signed at London, May 1, 1945, 5 U.S.T. 2062, T.I.A.S. No. 3070, 236 U.N.T.S. 400, in Documents on Germany, 1944-1959, at 10.

[8]Agreement, *supra* note 7, art. 1.

[9]*Id.*, art. 3, paras. (a) and (c).

[10]*Id.*, art. 3, para. (b).

[11]*Id.*, art. 10.

[12]Communiqué Issued at the End of the [Yalta] Conference, Feb. 11, 1945, in U.S. Dep't of State, Foreign Relations of the United States: The Conferences at Malta and Yalta 1945, 968, 970 (1955).

[13]A Decade of American Foreign Policy 506, 512, Documents on Germany, 1944-1959, 13, 18.

[14]Identic Notes from the Governments of the United Kingdom and the United States Addressed to the Government of the Union of Soviet Socialist Republics, July 6, 1948, Note from the Government of the French Republic Addressed to the Government of the Union of Soviet Socialist Republics, July 6, 1948, in *Germany: An Account of the Events Leading Up to a Reference of the Berlin Question to the United Nations*, Germany No. 2 (1948), Cmd. No. 7534, at 47, 49 (1948) [hereinafter cited as Germany No. 2 (1948), Cmd. No. 7534], U.S. Dep't of State, Germany, 1947-1949: The Story in Documents 205 (1950) [hereinafter cited as Germany 1947-1949]. Mosely's account of the drafting in meetings of the European Advisory Commission in 1944 of the agreements on future zones of occupation in Germany and sectors of occupation in Berlin, *The Occupation of Germany*, 28 Foreign Affairs 580 (1950), would seem to confirm that there was an assumption and acceptance there of the principle of free and independent access to their Berlin sectors for the two (later three) Western powers. He writes that the first week of April, 1944 President Roosevelt had authorized John G. Winant, the American representative to the European Advisory Commission, to approve the Soviet zone proposed by the British representative on January 15, 1944 and accepted by the Soviet representative on February 18, 1944. Winant informed his colleagues orally of this position, but refrained from presenting it in writing

> since he assumed that Washington would want to see some arrangements concerning access to Berlin included. At this time, of course, it was assumed that such provisions would relate only to the personnel and matériel of the armed forces, since planning was proceeding on the assumption that Germany herself would be treated as a political and economic unit and therefore no special provisions would be needed to regulate the economic relations between Berlin and any of the zones.

Id. at 593. In his discussions in the U.S. War Department Winant offered to propose that the Protocol on zones of occupation contain detailed provisions safeguarding American access to Berlin by highway, railroad and air.

> Since the Soviet representative had repeatedly insisted that there would be no difficulty in arranging for transit through the Soviet zone to Berlin, and that the presence of American and British forces in Berlin "of course" carried with it all necessary facilities of access, Mr. Winant was confident that concrete provisions could be negotiated in the EAC without great difficulty.

Id. at 592-93. However the War Department component of the inter-departmental committee which provided the American representative to the European Advisory Commission with his government's instructions insisted that access to Berlin was a purely "military matter" which would be taken care of "at the military level" when the time came. Winant felt that he could not further challenge this authoritative military view. *Id.* at 593. On the reason for the omission from the E.A.C. agreements of specific provisions regarding access to Berlin, Mosely's possibly more authoritative account differs somewhat from that in Clay, Decision in Germany 15 (1950).

[15]From April 18 until June 13, 1945 Prime Minister Churchill was to urge President Truman that the United States and the United Kingdom take advantage of this unexpected tactical deployment of Western troops to bring about a clarification of postwar Soviet and Western relations generally, and to effect agreements with the U.S.S.R. on particular problems of occupation in Germany and Austria. He suggested that British and American forces remain on the lines to which they had advanced at the end of German resistance, rather than withdraw to the zones prescribed in the occupation agreements, until these problems were settled between the Western and Soviet powers. See 6 Churchill, The Second World War: Triumph and Tragedy 443-52, 522-28 (1954); 1 Truman, Memoirs: Year of Decisions 60-61, 210-19, 297-304 (1955). But Truman maintained that the tripartite agreements about the occupation of Germany made it impossible to delay the withdrawal of American troops from the Soviet zone in order to press the settlement of other problems. Further, he was advised that the Soviets might insist upon such withdrawal as a corollary to the establishment of the Allied Control Council on a functioning basis in Berlin and to turning over the several sectors in Berlin to the Western occupation forces. See 6 Churchill, *op. cit. supra,* at 525; 1 Truman, *op. cit. supra,* at 298-303.

[16]See 1 Truman, *op. cit. supra* note 15, at 302; Clay, Decision in Germany 22-23 (1950).

[17]1 Truman, *op. cit. supra* note 15, at 305, Documents on Germany, 1944-1959, 441.

[18]6 Churchill, *op. cit. supra* note 15, at 526.

[19]1 Truman, *op. cit. supra* note 15, at 305, Documents on Germany, 1944-1959, 441; 6 Churchill, *op. cit. supra* note 15, at 527.

[20]Clay, Decision in Germany 25-26 (1950). In the statement made before the U.N. Security Council on October 6, 1948 by Philip C. Jessup, Deputy U.S. Representative to the Security Council, Marshal Zhukov is quoted as having said further at that June 29th meeting, in reply to a question from General Clay:

> It will be necessary for vehicles to be governed by Russian road signs, military police, document checking; but there will be no inspection of cargo — the USSR is not interested in what is being hauled, how much or how many trucks are moving.

U.N. Security Council Off. Rec. 3d year, 363d meeting 1, 7(S/PV.115) (1948), 19 Dep't State Bull. 485 (1948).

[21]Allied Agreement on the Quadripartite Administration of Berlin, 1945: Resolution of the Conference of the Representatives of the Allied Commands on the Joint Administration of Berlin, July 7, 1945.

[22]See Clay, Decision in Germany 29 (1950); Documents on Germany, 1944-1959, 442.

[23]See Clay, Decision in Germany 27-29 (1950); Howley, Berlin Command 57-59 (1950).

[24]See Clay, Decision in Germany 30 (1950). When on June 24, 1948 Soviet authorities halted all food and coal rail shipments from the West to Berlin, they also issued orders prohibiting the distribution of any supplies from the Soviet zone and sector to any of the western sectors of Berlin. Not until July 20, 1948, when the Western airlift was in successful operation, did Soviet authorities offer to supply food to the civilian inhabitants of the western sectors of the city, upon onerous conditions. See Statement before the U.N. Security Council on October 6, 1948 by Philip C. Jessup, Deputy U.S. Representative to the Security Council, U.N. Security Council Off. Rec. 3d year, 363d meeting 1, 4-5, 15 (S/PV. 115) (1948). Supply of the subsistence needs of civilians in West Berlin and other economic support has in practice been furnished by the Federal Republic of Germany at least since 1952. See note 104 *infra*.

[25]Plischke, Berlin: Development of Its Government and Administration 2-3, 211 (1952). See Documents on Germany, 1944-1959, 442.

[26]Protocol of the Proceedings of the Berlin (Potsdam) Conference, Aug. 1, 1945, part I, sec. A, subpara. (3) (i), A Decade of American Foreign Policy 34, Documents on Germany, 1944-1959, 24, 25.

[27]Potsdam Protocol, Part II, sec. A, subpara. 9 (iv), *id.* at 37, Documents on Germany, 1944-1959, 28.

[28]Potsdam Protocol, Part II, sec. B, para. 14, *id.* at 38, Documents on Germany, 1944-1959, 28-29.

[29]Official Gazette of the Control Council for Germany 4.

[30]*Cf.* Letter from the Foreign Minister of the German Democratic Republic to the Deputy Foreign Minister of the Soviet Union, Sept. 20, 1955, confirming that "the transportation of military personnel or of garrison material of the troops of the three Western Powers in West Berlin will be permitted on the basis of existing Four-Power decisions: (A) On the Autobahn Berlin-Marienborn, (B) On the Railway Line Berlin-Helmstedt,...(C) In the air corridors Berlin-Hamburg, Berlin-Bueckeburg, and Berlin-Frankfurt-Main," in Documents on Germany, 1944-1959, 158.

[31]Report of the Air Directorate, Allied Control Authority, Concerning the Creation of a System of Air Corridors to be Used for Flights in the Respective Zones of Occupation in Germany, submitted to the Coordinating Committee, Nov. 22, 1945 (CORC/P(45)170), and to the Control Council, Nov. 28, 1945 (CONL/P-(45)63). The Control Council approved the establishment of three air corridors from Berlin to the Western zones as defined in CONL/P(45)63, on November 30, 1945, Item 110(a), CONL/M(45)13, at 6. See Note from the United States to the Soviet Union, Sept. 8, 1961, documenting the Western position on unrestricted air access to Berlin, 45 Dep't State Bull. 511 (1961).

[32]See, *e.g.*, in Documents on Germany, 1944-1959, the entries for March 6-22, 1951, at 470, and October 23, 1952, at 478.

[33]See Statement before the U.N. Security Council, Oct. 6, 1948, by Philip C. Jessup, Deputy U.S. Representative to the Security Council, U.N. Security Council Off. Rec. 3d year, 363d meeting 1, 9 (S/PV.115) (1948), 19 Dep't State Bull. 485, 486 (1948).

[34]See Nettl, The Eastern Zone and Soviet Policy in Germany, 1945-50, 260-63 (1951). The author remarks that civilian passenger transit into the Soviet zone from the West before the institution of a pass system took place with any kind of spurious authority, and generally with no authority at all. In 1946 the Control Council established liberal procedures by which German civilians might obtain one-trip interzonal passes without preliminary sanction of the commanding authorities of the zone to be visited. The directive was amended on April 23, 1947 to extend the time period for which a pass might be issued, and the reasons for which a pass would be allowed. Official Gazette of the Control Council for Germany 274.

[35]See Nettl, *op. cit. supra* note 34, at 184-91, 273-77.

[36]Witness the successive restrictions on commercial passenger and freight traffic moving to and from Berlin which began to be imposed by Soviet authorities on April 3, 1948 and which culminated on June 23, 1948 in total land blockade, Documents on Germany, 1944-1959, 445-47.

[37]CORC/P(46)84; DAIR/M(46)11. See further Note from the United States to the U.S.S.R., Sept. 8, 1961, documenting the Western position on unrestricted air access to Berlin, 45 Dep't State Bull. 511, 512 (1961); Text of Soviet Report, Feb. 5, 1947, on Flights of Allied Aircraft Over German Territory, prepared in connection with the 1947 meeting in Moscow of the Council of Foreign Ministers, id. at 477.

[38]See Bathurst & Simpson, Germany and the North Atlantic Community: A Legal Survey 51-52, 56-57 (1956); Clay, Decision in Germany 120-62 passim (1950).

[39]The offer was made by U.S. Secretary of State Byrnes on July 11, 1946 at the second session of the Council of Foreign Ministers, and was reiterated in his address at Stuttgart on September 6, 1946. The American representative submitted the proposal to the Control Council for Germany on July 20, 1946. See Report by U.S. Secretary of State Byrnes on the second part of the second meeting of the Council of Foreign Ministers, July 15, 1946, A Decade of American Foreign Policy 79, 85; Stuttgart Address by U.S. Secretary of State Byrnes, Sept. 6, 1946, Documents on Germany, 1944-1959, 35, 38; Note from the U.S. Department of State to the Soviet Ambassador at Washington, March 26, 1948, in Germany 1947-1949, 85.

[40]Memorandum of Agreement between the United States and the United Kingdom relating to the economic fusion of American and British zones of occupation in Germany, done at Washington, Dec. 2, 1946, 61 Stat. 2475, T.I.A.S. No. 1575, 7 U.N.T.S. 163, in A Decade of American Foreign Policy 528.

[41]See, e.g., Stuttgart Address by U.S. Secretary of State Byrnes, Sept. 6, 1946, in Documents on Germany, 1944-1959, 35, 38.

[42]See, e.g., Note from the Soviet Government to the Governments of the United Kingdom, the United States, and France, March 6, 1948, in U.S.S.R. Ministry of Foreign Affairs, The Soviet Union and the Berlin Question (Documents) 7 (1948).

[43]See Report by U. S. Secretary of State Marshall on the fifth Session of the Council of Foreign Ministers, Dec. 19, 1947, in Germany 1947—1949, 63, Documents on Germany, 1944-1959, 51.

[44]See London Six-Power Conference, February 23-June 2, 1948, Communiqués and Recommendations, in Germany 1947-1949, 75. Documents on Germany, 1944-1959, 56.

[45]Notes from the Soviet Government to the Governments of the United States, the United Kingdom, and France, Feb. 13, 1948 and

March 6, 1948, in U.S.S.R. Ministry of Foreign Affairs, The Soviet Union and the Berlin Question (Documents) 5, 7 (1948).

[46]Notes from the U.S. Department of State to the Soviet Ambassador at Washington, Feb. 21, 1948 and March 26, 1948, in Germany 1947-1949, 84.

[47]See Clay, Decision in Germany 355-56 (1950); Germany 1947-1949, 200; U.S.S.R. Ministry of Foreign Affairs, The Soviet Union and the Berlin Question (Documents) 18 (1948).

[48]On March 25, 1948 U.S. Secretary of State Marshall was to say of the withdrawal of the Soviet military governor from meetings of the Allied Control Council:

> The ACC in Berlin as well as the joint occupation of the city are established by governmental agreement. Any further attempt to disrupt the functioning of the Allied Control Authority, as initially suggested by the conduct of the Soviet representative on March 20, could only be construed as reflecting an intention, which the United States does not share, to renounce efforts to obtain Four Power agreement on policies for Germany and would be regarded as unilateral action aimed against the unification of Germany. In accordance with the international agreement binding on all four control powers, the United States intends to continue to fulfill its responsibilities as a member of the Control Council and as a joint occupant of the city of Berlin.

Germany 1947-1949, 200-01, Documents on Germany, 1944-1959, 444. *But see* Bathurst & Simpson, Germany and the North Atlantic Community: A Legal Survey 79, 185 (1956), who suggest that the Soviet withdrawal from the Control Council, which made quadripartite exercise of supreme authority in Germany impossible, can only be construed as a repudiation of the Agreement on Control Machinery in Germany, and that the Western occupying powers "undoubtedly" acquiesced in the repudiation, for at the sixth session of the Council of Foreign Ministers, May 23-June 20, 1949, they made it clear that they would not contemplate any resumption of quadripartite control in Germany requiring decisions by unanimous vote. See further *Report on the Proceedings of the Sixth Session of the Council of Foreign Ministers, Paris, May 23-June 20, 1949*, Miscellaneous No. 11 (1949), Cmd. No. 7729, at 3, 7 (1949).

[49]See U.S. Dep't of State, The Berlin Crisis: A Report on the Moscow Discussions 1948, 1-5 (1948), Germany 1947-1949, 202-04.

[50]Letter from Marshal Sokolovsky, Soviet Military Governor, to General Robertson, British Military Governor, June 25, 1948, in U.S.S.R.

Ministry of Foreign Affairs. The Soviet Union and the Berlin Question (Documents) 30 (1948).

[51]See Walter Bedell Smith, My Three Years in Moscow 242-51 (1950).

[52]See Nettl, The Eastern Zone and Soviet Policy in Germany 1945-50, 107-08 (1951).

[53]Id. at 108.

[54]Id. at 108-09.

[55]See Clay, Decision in Germany, 208-11, 362 (1950).

[56]Law No. 61, First Law for Monetary Reform, Military Government Gazette, Germany, U.S. Zone, Issue J, Aug. 1, 1948, p. 6. See Clay, Decision in Germany 363 (1950): U.S.S.R. Ministry of Foreign Affairs, The Soviet Union and the Berlin Question (Documents) 25 (1948); Documents on Germany, 1944-1959, 446.

[57]Letters from Marshal Sokolovsky to General Clay, June 20, 1948, June 22, 1948, to General Robertson, June 25, 1948, in U.S.S.R. Ministry of Foreign Affairs, The Soviet Union and the Berlin Question (Documents) 25, 28, 30 (1948).

[58]See id. at 29. Documents on Germany, 1944-1959, 446.

[59]See Clay, Decision in Germany 364-65 (1950).

[60]Documents on Germany, 1944-1959, 447-51 *passim*. See further Nettl, *op. cit. supra* note 52, at 276.

[61]See Walter Bedell Smith, My Three Years in Moscow 238-53 (1950); Clay, Decision in Germany 369-71 (1950); U.S. Dep't of State, The Berlin Crisis: A Report on the Moscow Discussions 1948 (1948).

[62]See documents in Germany 1947-1949, 219-74.

[63]See Mosely, *The Occupation of Germany*, 28 Foreign Affairs 580, 593 (1950), and note 14 *supra*.

[64]See Identic Notes from the Governments of the United States and the United Kingdom Addressed to the Government of the Union of Soviet Socialist Republics, July 6, 1948, in Germany No. 2 (1948). Cmd. No. 7534, at 48, 19 Dep't State Bull. 85 (1948); Statements before the U.N. Security Council on October 6, 1948 by Philip C. Jessup, Deputy U.S. Representative in the Security Council, and Sir Alexander Cadogan, United Kingdom Representative in the Security Council, U.N Security Off. Rec. 3d year, 363d and 364th meetings 1, 4-5, 9, 15 and 27, 29, 32 (S/PV.115) (1948).

[65]See Nettl, *op. cit. supra* note 52, at 276-77.

[66]Agreement between the United States, the United Kingdom, France, and the U.S.S.R. relating to the lifting of restrictions imposed since March 1, 1948, on communications, transportation, and trade with Berlin, dated at New York, May 4, 1949, 63 Stat. 2410, T.I.A.S. No. 1915, 138 U.N.T.S. 123, in Documents on Germany, 1944-1959, 59.

[67]Communiqué on the Sixth Session of the Council of Foreign Ministers, June 20, 1949, para. 5, Germany 1947-1949, 69-70, Documents on Germany, 1944-1959, 64.

[68]See Howley, Berlin Command 179-82 (1950); Germany 1947-1949, 201.

[69]Documents on Germany, 1944-1959, 451-57 *passim.*

[70]See Basic Law for the Federal Republic of Germany, promulgated May 23, 1949, Germany 1947-1949, 283; Basic Law as amended, effective March 15, 1955, in 2 Peaslee, Constitutions of Nations 30 (2d ed. 1956). The preamble of the Basic Law declares that in enacting it the German people of the western *Länder* had acted also "on behalf of those Germans to whom participation was denied." Article 23 provides that accession to the Basic Law is open to "other parts of Germany."

[71]Agreements between the United States, the United Kingdom, and France relating to basic principles for the merger of the three Western German zones of occupation and other matters, signed at Washington, April 8, 1949, Occupation Statute, 63 Stat. 2817, T.I.A.S. No. 2066, 140 U.N.T.S. 196, in A Decade of American Foreign Policy 585, 586, Germany 1947-1949, 89.

[72]Supreme Allied Authority in the Federal Republic of Germany: Charter of the Allied High Commission, June 20, 1949, in A Decade of American Foreign Policy 603, Germany 1947-1949, 92.

[73]Agreed Memorandum regarding the principles governing exercise of powers and responsibilities of U.S.-U.K.-French Governments following establishment of German Federal Republic, para. 1, *supra* note 71.

[74]Agreement as to Tripartite Controls, *supra* note 71.

[75]Protocol between the United States, the United Kingdom, France, and the Federal Republic of Germany on the termination of the occupation régime in the Federal Republic of Germany, with five schedules and related letters, signed at Paris, Oct. 23, 1954, 6 U.S.T. 4117, T.I.A.S. No. 3425, 331 U.N.T.S. 253.

[76]Convention between the United Kingdom, the United States, France, and the Federal Republic of Germany on Relations between the Three Powers and the Federal Republic of Germany, signed at Bonn, May 26, 1952 (as amended by Schedule I to the Protocol on the Termination of the Occupation Régime in the Federal Republic of Germany, signed at Paris, Oct. 23, 1954), art. 1, para. 2, 6 U.S.T. 4251, T.I.A.S. No. 3425, 331 U.N.T.S. 327.

[77]Convention on Relations, *supra* note 76, art. 2 and art. 4, para. 2.

[78]Protocol to the North Atlantic Treaty on the accession of the Federal Republic of Germany, signed at Paris, Oct. 23, 1954, 6 U.S.T.

5707, T.I.A.S. No. 3428, 243 U.N.T.S. 308, in Documents on Germany, 1944-1959, 142.

[79]Exchange of letters between Premier Bulganin of the U.S.S.R. and Chancellor Adenauer of the Federal Republic of Germany, Sept. 13, 1955, in Documents on Germany, 1944-1959, 155, 156.

[80]See Nettl, The Eastern Zone and Soviet Policy in Germany, 1945-50, 111-13 (1951); Simpson, *Berlin: Allied Rights and Responsibilities in the Divided City*, 6 Int'l & Comp. L.Q. 83, 98-99 (1957).

[81]See Nettl, *op. cit. supra* note 80, at 112, Documents on Germany, 1944-1959, 463.

[82]Treaty between the Soviet Union and the German Democratic Republic, signed at Moscow, Sept. 20, 1955, in Documents on Germany, 1944-1959, 156.

[83]Letter from the Foreign Minister of the German Democratic Republic to the Deputy Foreign Minister of the Soviet Union, Sept. 20, 1955, in Documents on Germany, 1944-1959, 158.

[84]See Bathurst & Simpson, Germany and the North Atlantic Community: A Legal Survey 199 (1956); Note from the Soviet Foreign Ministry to the American Embassy, on the Soviet-GDR Agreements, Oct. 18, 1955, in Documents on Germany, 1944-1959, 159.

[85]Treaty of Friendship, Cooperation, and Mutual Assistance between Albania, Bulgaria, Hungary, the German Democratic Republic, Poland, Rumania, the U.S.S.R., and Czechoslovakia, done at Warsaw, May 14, 1955, in Documents on Germany, 1944-1959, 144.

[86]See Communiqué by the Foreign Ministers of the United States, the United Kingdom, and France, Sept. 19, 1950, 1 U.S. Dep't of State, American Foreign Policy 1950-1955: Basic Documents 1462 (1957) [hereinafter cited as American Foreign Policy 1950-1955]; Joint Declaration by the Allied High Commission on the Status of East Germany, April 8, 1954, 30 Dep't State Bull. 588 (1954), Documents on Germany, 1944-1959, 123. Compare the letter from Chancellor Adenauer to Premier Bulganin, Sept. 13, 1955, stating certain reservations at the time of establishing diplomatic relations between the U.S.S.R. and the Federal Republic of Germany, in Documents on Germany, 1944-1959, 156.

[87]See, *e.g.*, in Documents on Germany, 1944-1959, the entries for May 15-19, 1949, at 460; July 8-14, 1949, at 461; January 26, 1950 and February 10-March 2, 1950, at 465; September 25, 1950, at 469; March 6-22, 1951, at 470; and June 16, 1951, at 471. Even American and British military traffic on the Berlin-Marienborn Autobahn was interrupted from May 8 to May 16, 1952, *id.* at 474. Civil and military flights in the Berlin air corridors continued to be rigorously tracked by Soviet author-

ities, but now off-course flights elicited not Soviet notes of protest but armed attack by Soviet fighter planes. See, *e.g.*, in Documents on Germany, 1944-1959, the entries for April 20, 1952, at 474 (French civil aircraft); October 8-16, 1952, at 477 (American hospital plane); and March 12, 1953, at 479 (British bomber on training mission). See further *The Soviet Harassment Campaign in Germany: Correspondence Between Allied and Soviet Representatives*, 27 Dep't Bull. 311 (1952).

[88]Documents on Germany, 1944-1959, 465.

[89]See, *e.g.*, the exchange of correspondence in 1953 and 1954 between the Western High Commissioners in Germany and the Soviet Commissioner, on removal of interzonal barriers to the free movement of German nationals and goods between West Berlin and Western Germany and between Berlin and the Soviet zone, 29 Dep't State Bull. 391-92, 490-91 (1953), 30 *id.*, 508-11, 879-81 (1954), 2 American Foreign Policy 1950-1955, 1750-58. The Western High Commissioners rejected the Soviet proposal that these questions be referred to the governments of the German Democratic Republic and the Federal Republic of Germany for their decision, or to "all-German" committees. The Western Commissioners maintained that these were matters falling solely within the authority of the occupation powers. See also the exchange of correspondence between the Western and Soviet Commissioners in Germany in 1955 on the drastic increase in tolls on roads in the Soviet zone, affecting primarily vehicles registered in the Federal Republic and West Berlin, 32 Dep't State Bull. 648, 736, 834, 997 (1955), 2 American Foreign Policy 1950-1955, 1758-61. Although the Western High Commissioners contended that the rate increases were so exorbitant as to amount to interference with free access to Berlin, in violation of the four-power accords of May 4, 1949 and June 30, 1949, the Soviet Commissioner replied:

> [T]he question of tariffs on roads of the German Democratic Republic relates to the competence of the government of the German Democratic Republic, and it hence follows that it is up to the German Democratic Republic to settle the matter by means of immediate negotiations between appropriate representatives of the German Democratic Republic and the German Federal Republic.

32 Dep't State Bull. 824 (1955).

[90]Note from the American Embassy to the Soviet Foreign Ministry, on the Soviet-GDR Agreements, Oct. 3, 1955, in Documents on Germany, 1944-1959, 159. See also Statement by the American, British, and French Foreign Ministers, on the Soviet-GDR Agreements, Sept. 28, 1955, *id*, at 158; and the further exchange of correspondence be-

tween the Soviet Foreign Ministry and the American Embassy on Oct. 18, 1955 and Oct. 27, 1955, *id.* at 159, 161.

[91]See Remarks to the Press by U.S. Secretary of State Dulles, Dec. 6, 1955, 2 American Foreign Policy 1950-1955, 1765; Remarks at News Conference by U.S. Secretary of State Dulles, on Berlin, Nov. 26, 1958, Documents on Germany, 1944-1959, 312-17; Statements at the 1959 Geneva Foreign Ministers Meeting by the West German Adviser, Mr. Grewe, and the East German Adviser, Mr. Bolz, in 1959 Geneva Foreign Ministers Meeting, at 545, 580, 595.

[92]See *supra* note 91. *Cf.* Western Proposal on Berlin, Handed to Foreign Minister Gromyko on June 16, 1959, subpara. 1(b):

> The Ministers agreed that there shall continue to be free and unrestricted access to West Berlin by land, by water and by air for all persons, goods and communications, including those of the French, United Kingdom and United States forces stationed in West Berlin. The procedures applicable shall be those in effect in April 1959. However, without prejudice to existing basic responsibilities, these procedures may where it is not already the case be carried out by German personnel.

Id. at 312, 41 Dep't State Bull. 153 (1959).

[93]Not without harassment, however. See Note from the American Embassy to the Soviet Foreign Ministry, Feb. 4, 1959, protesting detention of a United States Army convoy, in Documents on Germany, 1944-1959, 380; Binder, *Communist Pressure Rises Along Berlin Wall*, N.Y. Times, Dec. 31, 1961, §E, p. 4, col. 1.

[94]See Plischke, Berlin: Development of Its Government and Administration 3-4, 160-64 (1952).

[95]Germany 1947-1949, 201. See also Howley, Berlin Command, 179-82 (1950).

[96]Plischke, *op. cit. supra* note 94, at 42-43, 212.

[97]Documents on Germany, 1944-1959, 60.

[98]*Id.* at 62.

[99]2 American Foreign Policy 1950-1955, 1740, Documents on Germany, 1944-1959, 100.

[100]See generally Plischke, *op. cit. supra* note 94, at 111-34.

[101]Article 23 of the Basic Law of the Federal Republic includes Greater Berlin among the *Länder* in which the Basic Law shall apply. But in approving the Basic Law the Western military governors stipulated that Article 23 was not to be interpreted as according to Berlin voting membership in the Bundestag or Bundesrat, nor as meaning that Berlin was to be governed by the Federation. Letter from the Three Western Military Governors to the President of the Parliamentary Coun-

cil, May 12, 1949, Germany 1947-1949, 279. The Allied Kommandatura has imposed similar restrictions on articles of the Berlin City Constitution of 1950 which declare that Berlin is a *Land* of the Federal Republic upon which the Basic Law and Federal laws are binding. See Simpson, *Berlin: Allied Rights and Responsibilities in the Divided City*, 6 Int'l & Comp. L.Q. 83, 91-93 (1957); Plischke, *op. cit. supra* note 94, at 117-19; Documents on Germany, 1944-1959, 468, 473, 488.

[102]See Plischke, *op. cit. supra* note 94, at 114-16, 121-23. The Federal Republic of Germany formally regards Berlin as the capital of a future reunited Germany, holds occasional symbolic meetings of its Bundesrat in West Berlin, and in 1954 and 1959 had the Federal Electoral College meet in West Berlin to elect the President of the Federal Republic. The U.S.S.R. charges that these and other visits to West Berlin by Federal Republic officials have as their purpose illegal and inadmissible interference in the affairs of West Berlin and subversion directed against the G.D.R. and the Soviet Union; in permitting them, Western occupying authorities abuse what privileges they enjoy in West Berlin through Soviet observance of a special status for the city. The U.S.S.R. further charges that the Western occupying authorities, in permitting the use of the air corridors for the transit of these West German officials, violate a four-power agreement that the corridors were to be used only for the needs of the military garrisons in Berlin. See the statements of Soviet Foreign Minister Gromyko and U.S. Secretary of State Herter at the 1959 Geneva Foreign Ministers Meeting, 1959 Geneva Foreign Ministers Meeting, at 389, 392-93 and 400-01; Exchange of Correspondence between the United States and the Soviet Union, Aug. 18-Sept. 8, 1961, 45 Dep't State Bull. 397, 431, 433, 511, 513 (1961).

[103]See Plischke, *op cit. supra* note 94, at 126-32, 231.

[104]On June 24, 1949 the American-British Economic Council of the Bizonal Economic Area decided to include West Berlin in this area, Documents on Germany, 1944-1959, 461. In negotiating interzonal trade agreements with East Germany, West Germany has since October, 1949 acted for West Berlin as well. See *id.* at 463. On November 7, 1949 the Federal Republic agreed to incorporate West Berlin's estimates for Marshall Plan aid in all future Federal estimates. *Ibid.* Annexed to the Bonn Convention on Relations, *supra* note 76, is a Declaration on Aid to Berlin by the German Federal Republic which, after reciting that Berlin is in special need of assistance from the Federation, gives an undertaking to continue the economic and political support already extended to Berlin by the Federal Republic. Documents on Germany, 1944-1959, 99. See generally Schmidt, Economic Assistance to West Berlin, 1949-1951 (1952).

[105]See Plischke, *op. cit. supra* note 94, at 131-34; Documents on Germany, 1944-1959, 473, 475; Letter from the American, British, and French High Commissioners to Chancellor Adenauer, on Aid to Berlin, May 26, 1952, *id.* at 98.

[106]See Plischke, *op. cit. supra* note 94, at 124-25; Simpson, *supra* note 101, at 93.

[107]*E.g.*, Final Act of the London Nine-Power Conference, Oct. 3, 1954, part V, 1 American Foreign Policy 1950-1955, 1474, 1482-83; Resolution of the North Atlantic Council, Oct. 22, 1954, in U.S. Dep't of State, London and Paris Agreements, September-October 1954, 36 (1954).

[108]See Western Peace Plan, Presented by the Foreign Ministers of France, the United Kingdom, and the United States, May 14, 1959, 1959 Geneva Foreign Ministers Meeting, at 55.

[109]See, *e.g.*, Exchange of Correspondence between the United States and the U.S.S.R., Aug. 17 and 18, 1961, on the closing of the Soviet sector border in Berlin, 45 Dep't State Bull. 396 (1961); Exchange of correspondence between the United States and the U.S.S.R. concerning the incidents of December 21 and 23, 1961, when East German police demanded identifying documents from civilian officials of the American command in Berlin entering the Soviet sector in U.S. Army vehicles for prearranged meetings with Soviet authorities, reported in N.Y. Times, Dec. 24, 1961, §1, p. 1, col. 8; Dec. 26, 1961, p. 3, col. 5; Jan 1, 1962, p. 1, col. 6; Jan. 4, 1962, p. 3, col. 1.

[110]See Binder, *Communist Pressure Rises Along Berlin Wall*, N.Y Times, Dec. 31, 1961, §E, p. 4, col. 1.

[111]See Documents on Germany, 1944-1959, 456, and note 69 *supra*.

[112]Civilian officials of the British command in Berlin show identity cards to the East German guards; American civilian officials have turned away rather than do so. See *supra* notes on 109 and 110.

[113]The Electoral Law enacted by the East German Provisional People's Chamber on August 9, 1950 provided in Article 49 that "the capital of Berlin sends to the People's Chamber 66 delegates with advisory vote." Documents on Germany, 1944-1959, 468. The Electoral Law of September 24, 1958 no longer specifies "advisory vote," but does distinguish in section 6 between the 400 *Mitglieder* who shall be chosen for the People's Chamber and the 66 *Vertreter* whom the capital of Berlin is entitled to send to the People's Chamber. [1958] 1 Gesetzblatt 677 (Ger. Dem. Rep.). The East German law of November 8, 1950 on the Composition of the *Länderkammer* of the German Democratic Republic did not include Berlin among the *Länder* whose *Abgeordneten* were to compose the *Länderkammer*, but it did provide that the capital of Berlin might send thirteen *Vertreter* with advisory vote.

[1950] 2 *id.* 1135. These limitations on representation may but mark the special position of the capital of a federal State, but since December 8, 1958, when in pursuance of "democratic centralism" the *Länderkammer* was dissolved and constitutional provisions concerning it abrogated, the German Democratic Republic has been in effect a unitary State. [1958] 1 *id.* 867. See further the statement of U.S. Secretary of State Herter on May 26, 1959 at the 1959 Geneva Foreign Ministers Meeting, 1959 Geneva Foreign Ministers Meeting, at 207, 213.

[114]Note from the Soviet Foreign Ministry to the American Ambassador at Moscow, regarding Berlin, Nov. 27, 1958, 40 Dep't State Bull. 81, 87 (1959), Documents on Germany, 1944-1959, 317, 328.

[115]*Supra* note 114.

[116]Note from the United States to the Soviet Union, Dec. 31, 1958, 40 Dep't State Bull. 79 (1959), Documents on Germany, 1944-1959, 347. See also Communiqué on Berlin by the Foreign Ministers of the United States, the United Kingdom, France, and the Federal Republic of Germany, Dec. 14, 1958, in U.S. Dep't of State, The Soviet Note on Berlin: An Analysis 50 (1959), Documents on Germany, 1944-1959, 33.

[117]Soviet authorities and the U.S.S.R. have since 1948 asserted that Greater Berlin is part of the territory of the Soviet zone in Germany. See note 57 *supra* and accompanying text. The further legal basis for the contention has since been supplied by Soviet and East German lawyers. See, *e.g.,* the article by Tunkin in Izvestia, February 18, 1960, summarized in Speier, Divided Berlin 76-78 (1961); Kroeger, *Proposals for the Peaceful Solution of the Berlin Question,* [1959] Law and Legislation in the German Democratic Republic 20, 24-26.

[118]On self-defense and necessity in international law, see Cheng, General Principles of Law as Applied by International Courts and Tribunals 69-102 (1953).

[119]See further Bathurst & Simpson, Germany and the North Atlantic Community: A Legal Survey 71-79, 184-95 (1956).

[120]E.g., the reservations with respect to rights and obligations of the Soviet Union regarding Germany as a whole contained in the treaty of September 20, 1955 between the U.S.S.R. and the German Democratic Republic and its accompanying instruments, *supra* notes 82-84 and accompanying text; the "Summit Statement" of July 23, 1955 recognizing "common responsibility for the settlement of the German question and the re-unification of Germany by means of free elections," Geneva Directive of the Heads of Government of the Four Powers to the Foreign Ministers, July 23, 1955, in Documents on Germany, 1944-1959, 153.